ROUTLEDGE LIBRARY EDITIONS: LIBRARY AND INFORMATION SCIENCE

Volume 24

CREATIVE PLANNING FOR LIBRARY ADMINISTRATION

CREATIVE PLANNING FOR LIBRARY ADMINISTRATION
Leadership for the Future

Edited by
KENT HENDRICKSON

LONDON AND NEW YORK

First published in 1991 by The Haworth Press, Inc.

This edition first published in 2020
by Routledge
2 Park Square, Milton Park, Abingdon, Oxon OX14 4RN

and by Routledge
52 Vanderbilt Avenue, New York, NY 10017

Routledge is an imprint of the Taylor & Francis Group, an informa business

© 1991 The Haworth Press, Inc.

All rights reserved. No part of this book may be reprinted or reproduced or utilised in any form or by any electronic, mechanical, or other means, now known or hereafter invented, including photocopying and recording, or in any information storage or retrieval system, without permission in writing from the publishers.

Trademark notice: Product or corporate names may be trademarks or registered trademarks, and are used only for identification and explanation without intent to infringe.

British Library Cataloguing in Publication Data
A catalogue record for this book is available from the British Library

ISBN: 978-0-367-34616-4 (Set)
ISBN: 978-0-429-34352-0 (Set) (ebk)
ISBN: 978-0-367-42084-0 (Volume 24) (hbk)
ISBN: 978-0-367-42089-5 (Volume 24) (pbk)
ISBN: 978-0-367-82171-5 (Volume 24) (ebk)

Publisher's Note
The publisher has gone to great lengths to ensure the quality of this reprint but points out that some imperfections in the original copies may be apparent.

Disclaimer
The publisher has made every effort to trace copyright holders and would welcome correspondence from those they have been unable to trace.

Creative Planning for Library Administration: Leadership for the Future

Kent Hendrickson
Editor

The Haworth Press
New York • London

Creative Planning for Library Administration: Leadership for the Future has also been published as *Journal of Library Administration*, Volume 14, Number 2.

© 1991 by The Haworth Press, Inc. All rights reserved. No part of this work may be reproduced or utilized in any form or by any means, electronic or mechanical, including photocopying, microfilm and recording, or by any information storage and retrieval system, without permission in writing from the publisher. Printed in the United States of America.

The Haworth Press, Inc. 10 Alice Street, Binghamton, NY 13904-1580
EUROSPAN/Haworth, 3 Henrietta Street, London WC2E 8LU England

Library of Congress Cataloging-in-Publication Data

Creative planning for library administration: leadership for the future / Kent Hendrickson, editor.
   p. cm.
   "Also . . . published as Journal of library administration, volume 14, number 2 1991" — T.p. verso.
   ISBN 1-56024-093-8 (acid free paper)
   1. Library administration 2. Library planning. I. Hendrickson, Kent.
Z678 C76
025. 1 — dc20   90-49103
                                                                                            CIP

Creative Planning for Library Administration: Leadership for the Future

CONTENTS

Introduction *Kent Hendrickson*	1

Building New Futures for Research Libraries
    Susan Jurow
    Duane E. Webster
	5

Performance Measures: A Tool for Planning Resource Allocations *Patricia M. Kelley*	21
Creating Your Library's Future Through Effective Strategic Planning *Brice G. Hobrock*	37
Creativity and Innovation in an Organized Anarchy *Joan R. Giesecke*	59
A New Leadership Paradigm: Empowering Library Staff and Improving Performance *Maureen Sullivan*	73
The Price of Partnership *Helen L. Gater*	87

Beyond Tomorrow: The Scholar, Libraries and the Dissemination of Information
    Irene Hoadley
    Sherrie Schmidt
	103

Introduction

Over the past fifteen years, the writings of Russell L. Ackoff have had a major influence on librarians and their approach to library management issues. One of the features of Ackoff's management philosophy, the interactive planning process, is based on the assumption that the future depends as much on what we do between now and then as it does on what happened until now. That is, the future is largely subject to creation and planning is a process that is used to help us create our own future. "Create our own future" is the key phrase and it serves as the foundation for this collection of articles.[1]

During the 1980's many academic librarians discovered that they can influence their library's future by making a formal planning process part of their way of doing business. For them planning became a routine task. It is also interesting to note that these same librarians often moved into leadership roles on their respective campuses. Through their own initiative they had an impact on campus governance, i.e., formal planning became a campus mode of operation. They helped establish the framework for influencing the future of the campus as well as that of the library.

Another aspect of this process of creating our own futures is creativity. If academic libraries are to build on their traditional role as information providers, they must come up with new and innovative ways to organize, access, and interpret the world's store of information. For the first time, libraries are up against competition for their services. Technology has made the library vulnerable. Planning is no longer enough. The development of mission statements, goals, and objectives by and of themselves will not get the job done. Creativity both in the work place and in the broader campus environment is required.

© 1991 by The Haworth Press, Inc. All rights reserved.

The following articles provide a variety of perspectives on the subjects of planning and creativity. The first three papers focus on the planning process. Susan Jurow and Duane Webster describe the Association of Research Libraries' Office of Management Services program for assisting libraries in the development of strategic plans. A critical tool used in the process, the design of a preferred future for the library, is featured. In the second paper, Pat Kelley, who has done pioneering work on the application of performance measures, presents the case for a measurement program. She emphasizes the need to determine how efficiently, how effectively, and how satisfactorily libraries are serving their clientele. In the third paper of this set, Brice Hobrock compares strategic planning to other planning methodologies. His paper provides us with an outline for the strategic planning process, and a summary of recent planning theory.

Creativity in the work place is the topic addressed in the next two papers. Joan Giesecke gives us all hope by describing the opportunities for creativity provided by unstable and ambiguous environments. Maureen Sullivan, based on her work with members of the Yale University Library staff, explains that the road to improved staff performance is through empowerment and meaningful involvement at all levels of the library organization.

The final two articles describe applications of innovation in academic library settings. Helen Gater relates elements of her library's unique partnership in academic affairs and the personal, professional, and organizational costs of pursuing such a partnership. Finally, Irene Hoadley and Sherrie Schmidt bring us up-to-date on the "electronic library." They warn that more research is needed before we can fully understand how today's scholar does his/her research.

The writers of several of the articles in this collection encourage the development of particular management styles. The others describe unique approaches to specific library issues. What they all have in common is the concept of creating the future. It is hoped that through these articles still others will be inspired to take control of their futures.

My special thanks go to Jan Medcalf whose long hours at her

word processor helped ensure the development of a quality product. Also to Joan Giesecke and Jean Williss who shared in the editorial effort.

Kent Hendrickson

NOTE

1. Russell L. Ackoff, *Creating the Corporate Future* (New York: John Wiley & Sons, 1981) p. 62.

Building New Futures for Research Libraries

Susan Jurow
Duane E. Webster

SUMMARY. Over the past six years, the Association of Research Libraries Office of Management Services (OMS) has worked with over 20 libraries to assist in the development of strategic plans. These efforts mark a change in the attitude of academic and research libraries towards their environment. This article will review key strategic planning concepts and outline the program developed by OMS to introduce strategic planning into academic and research libraries. A critical tool used in the process, the design of a preferred future for the library, will be highlighted.

Over the past six years, the Association of Research Libraries Office of Management Services (OMS) has worked with over 20 libraries to assist in the development of strategic plans. These efforts mark a change in the attitude of academic and research libraries towards their environment. Through the strategic planning process, these libraries and many others have taken the initiative to try to influence the shape of their future rather than just wait for it to happen. This article will review key strategic planning concepts and outline the program developed by OMS to introduce strategic planning into academic and research libraries. A critical tool used in the process, the design of a preferred future for the library, will be highlighted.

Susan Jurow is Director of the Association of Research Libraries Office of Management Studies, Washington, DC. Duane E. Webster is Director of the Association of Research Libraries, Washington, DC.

© 1991 by The Haworth Press, Inc. All rights reserved.

THE DYNAMIC ENVIRONMENT FACING LIBRARIES

Over the past twenty-five years, academic and research libraries have ridden the same roller coaster of change as the rest of American society. Periods of growth with substantial financial resources for educational enterprises have been followed by recessions that forced the cancellation of newly developed programs and services. Both internal and external pressures have played a role in creating this dynamic environment which has forced the rethinking and reshaping of traditional library strategies.

Economics

The largesse of the 1960's continues to haunt the not-for-profit sector. Resources currently available will always seem scarce in comparison with those of that period. After twenty years of shrinking project funds, libraries no longer expect or rely upon grants and outside funding. Energy has finally shifted from trying to get more money to determining how to make the best possible use of the resources at hand. It is difficult for those who work in libraries to see, however, how they will be able to undertake new initiatives within the framework of existing dollars.

Technology

"Technology" tends to be a catch-all word for a number of developments that have an impact on the higher education community. Multiplicity of information formats and the application of computer and communication technology to operations are two of the expensive dilemmas facing libraries. The information resources of libraries can be made available to users in new, more efficient and effective ways, but the price tag for these opportunities is steep. The decision to introduce technological refinements into libraries becomes a conscious choice that overrides the decision to put scarce financial resources to other uses.

Demographics

The user population and the workforce of libraries are changing in ways that are both parallel and complementary. An increasing number of people are returning to college after working for a period of time. Their expectation of what a library can and should offer is dictated by their experience in the workplace. Many are computer literate, and, along with undergraduates coming straight from high school who have grown up with computers, they expect to find a certain level of technological sophistication.

A more culturally and ethnically diverse user population needs and is seeking different kinds of assistance as it reaches institutions of higher learning. Libraries have a unique role to play in assisting in their educational process. In few academic and research libraries is this diversity reflected in the workplace. The recognition of the value of diversity as well as the need to encourage it is beginning to change the way in which these libraries recruit staff.

Culture and Values

The interest in diversity is one manifestation of changing values in society at large. People are questioning their work environment and their role in the workplace in relation to their personal goals. Libraries are starting to experiment with participative organizational structures such as self-managing work groups as a means of providing greater autonomy, flexibility and personal accountability. Both of these trends will have an effect on the kinds of training and staff development programs that libraries will have to offer in the future.

Economic, technological, demographic and sociological changes have had and continue to have an impact on the effectiveness of academic and research libraries. It has become clear that it will be a long time before academic and research libraries find themselves in a period stable enough to permit the use of an incremental approach to thinking about the future.

PLANNING AS AN ORGANIZATIONAL PROCESS

Planning is one of the critical activities of management because it is through the planning process that an organization determines its direction. Careful planning is needed to ensure effective use of resources, but uncertainty about the future makes it difficult to map a course for development. In the past, decisions about library programs and services could be based on previous experience. Today, it is difficult to know from one year to the next what kinds of resources will be available, what needs will have to be met or even what kind of staff will be available in libraries to carry out the mission.

Because of this ongoing turmoil, the nature and role of planning has changed for academic and research libraries over the past ten years as it has for many other enterprises. The planning function has traditionally provided a framework for organizational decision making through development of a mission statement, goal-setting and establishment of objectives. Because the environment in which libraries operate today can no longer be relied upon to behave in a linear or predictable fashion, libraries along with other organizations, have had to look for other ways of making decisions that will contribute to the long-term success of the institution.

Many libraries have turned to strategic planning as a way of balancing current and future needs. Strategic planning focuses organizational energy in a very different way. It is a "process by which the guiding members of an organization envision its future and develop the necessary procedures and operations to achieve the future."[1] The three key concepts in this definition are the guiding members, the vision, and the achievement of the future. Strategic planning requires the development of a vision of a desired and possible future by individuals who have the energy and drive to create in the present the means by which their version of the future can happen.

Strategic planning is built on careful analysis, but it relies heavily on intuition and creative insight. The process must include information about where the organization is and where it has been, as well as where it would like to go. It must also have leadership imbued with a strength of purpose and a willingness to lead in directions that may not seem appropriate when judged only by current standards and the current environment. The leap of faith required for this vision is often difficult for staff struggling with the realities of managing day-to-day operations with limited resources or users focused on their immediate needs.

There are three different modes for undertaking any kind of planned organizational change process: reactive, proactive, and interactive.[2] A planning process that is driven by current operations is a "reactive" model for change. It presupposes that the best course can be set by those actively involved in day-to-day activities because they are most in touch with current needs. A proactive change process identifies and engages those elements in the environment that will be key to a successful future. It assumes that the leadership of the organization can identify the right issues and be able to influence them in such a way that the desired outcome will be achieved.

The interactive model for change includes both bottom-up and top-down information and ideas. It demystifies the process by making it an open process, so that the antecedents of the final product, the vision of the future towards which the library will strive, are more clearly understood and accepted. As a result, the strategic planning process must reach inward and outward in order to be successful; it must encompass the library staff and the community of which the library is a part. By encouraging broad participation, library-wide and community-wide integration and commitment is much more likely to occur. The OMS Leadership Development Program is based upon this model for organizational change.

THE LEADERSHIP DEVELOPMENT PROGRAM

In early 1986, OMS developed, in partnership with Yale University Libraries, the Leadership Development Program (LDP). Designed as a three to four day retreat, the LDP provides an opportunity for senior managers to reflect on the issues affecting future development of library programs and services. By providing a forum for frank, open discussion of the current situation and the potential for change, the result is not only a better understanding of future directions the library might take, but also a commitment to undertaking a process that will lead to change. The retreat helps the library prepare to undertake a strategic planning process by simulating the steps.

Organizational Review

The program begins with a review of the library's history and traditions. This exercise helps to highlight the elements of the organizational culture that may affect future development. The factors vary from library to library. For example, the style of a particular director may have had a major impact at one library, while the physical facilities occupied over the course of time may have affected the programs and services that another library could offer. At still other libraries, critical events may have been dictated by changes in the university or local community.

An assessment of the environment and implications for the library is the second step in the LDP. Before making decisions that will affect the future, an inventory of external factors, including trends and stakeholders, is made. This step helps to clarify the relationship between the library and the world outside by identifying external threats and opportunities. The review includes consideration of forces in society at large, in higher education, and in technology, along with developments at the state, regional, or local level.

Because current capabilities provide the foundation for decisions about growth, maintenance, or downsizing of programs and services, the third step reviews the internal situation. It is designed to identify assumptions about current levels of performance, and it provides an opportunity to test consensus about perceived strengths and weaknesses. For example, one means of deciding where to deploy limited human or financial resources is to build on existing strengths rather than thinly spreading resources to cover all the possible initiatives.[3]

Internal climate and organizational values influence the ability of the library to engage in a change process and may dictate the kind of change process it is possible to undertake. The range of beliefs, attitudes and values surrounding the library as an enterprise, its fundamental *raison d'etre* and means of operation, are explored in the fourth step. By clarifying the various points of view and assumptions, conflict is less likely to occur as the process continues. This step can be difficult because these are issues that most individuals are not accustomed to thinking about or discussing with others.

Speculation about the Future

The review activities establish the base for speculation about the future. In the fifth step, the group is presented with four scenarios that represent four possible futures for academic and research libraries. The group examines the futures and assesses their likelihood and desirability based on the local environment and needs. Each possible future is discussed in terms of its strong points and weak points.

A subgroup or team is established to prepare a first draft of a scenario that reflects the needs and aspirations of that particular library based on the analysis of the previous steps. While the team is working, the rest of the group engages in other activities that focus on group decision making and strategy development. When completed the new scenario is discussed and modified. It is used as a working model for the rest of the retreat with the understanding that a more carefully crafted document will have to be created during the organizational strategic planning process.

Planning to Plan

In step six, the group examines the new scenario for key result areas. Also known as "critical success factors," key result areas are those "areas of activity that should receive constant and careful attention from management"[4] in order to ensure success of an enterprise. In a collection-driven research library, key result areas might be a continuous or increased level of materials funding and a close relationship to the faculty. In a service-driven library with an instructional mandate, key result areas might be high staffing levels and availability of technological innovations.

As the last stage of the retreat, the group discusses the construct of the local strategic planning process. Preliminary decisions are made about timing, participation, and data collection.

It is not possible to do strategic planning in three or four days. Unless a library has recently undertaken studies that can provide objective data, the results of the discussion in retreat reflect assumptions on the part of the library staff. These assumptions must be examined for accuracy and validity at a later point. Strategic planning is a project that requires the time and effort of a large body of staff. In the libraries with which OMS has worked, the actual strategic planning process has taken anywhere from 3 to 18 months depending on a number of factors: the depth of analysis needed or desired, the amount of data already available, staff time and energy, competing projects, etc.

ALTERNATIVE FUTURES FOR LIBRARIES

One of the key activities in the Leadership Development Program is the construction of a vision or scenario for the future. Other OMS programs have validated our experience that it is difficult for people to think about something that doesn't exist, to imagine a future that hasn't yet occurred. Individuals and groups will usually fall back on science fiction, and the responses are predictable, based on elements of books and articles that have been widely read.

The scenarios illustrate and clarify two key concepts—the importance of the vision and the capacity of organizations and individuals to influence the shape of the future. The word "vision" conjures up for many the idea of fantasy unrelated to reality. The scenarios demonstrate that it is possible to design a desired future based on present information that is not a direct projection of the present. Once that concept is understood and accepted, it is much easier for people to see their role in the implementation of that future.

In 1984, using as a model the scenarios created by Nina Matheson for the Medical Library Association,[5] the Association of Research Libraries Taskforce on Research Library Staffing designed four scenarios to use in discussions of the staffing needs of academic and research libraries for the coming decade. These organizational projections were constructed by first identifying those factors that would likely play a key role in the development of library programs and services, such as information technology, the university context, user expectations and capabilities, national information infrastructure, and library philosophy and role. Four different ways of approaching these factors were outlined—withdrawal, mirror reflection, selective engagement, and proactive initiative. The four scenarios reflect the futures that could result if a library chose to engage the factors in each of these four ways.

Option One

This library provides traditional physical and bibliographic access to published knowledge, employing some automated techniques to achieve needed economies. Primary sources are hard copy documents, with computerized bibliographic control provided for most collections owned. Telecommunication is used to provide supplementary access to required data files. Commercial automated information services are available on a fee basis.

Full public services are provided on an on-demand basis responding to specific requests for assistance, especially in the use of collection and the facility. The card catalog is closed, but limited retrospective conversion prevents a fully functioning on-line catalog. Staff are general purpose librarians with a fair amount of functional specialization.

Option Two

The library continues to center around the traditional functions of acquiring, housing, organizing, and making available printed resources that support the instructional and research missions of the university. The library has automated most functions and provides on-line bibliographic access to its collections as well as most of the nation's published literature. Online information services are provided for most subjects emphasized by the university. In addition, the library has assumed an information transfer role wherever it is available (extensive use is made of formal network and consortia arrangements) and provides this information to users regardless of academic status.

Information services are emphasized and aggressive outreach programs such as end user searching and information management education are operated. The library staff has a number of specialists, with most librarians operating with multiple responsibilities that cut across the traditional functions. Networks and cooperative arrangements are used extensively to provide backup support and achieve savings in bibliographic control and access to needed materials. The card catalog has been closed and retrospective conversion completed.

Option Three

The library evolves to a series of sophisticated discipline-oriented information services modeled after the medical field where national and regional services provide the infrastructure for local agencies to provide timely, user-tailored information support. Such service is available in the humanistic and historical studies, social science, physical sciences, biological sciences, and the prominent professional schools through decentralized, institutionalized information units.

Public services vary according to the characteristics and needs of the discipline but tend to be personalized and intense, relying extensively on technology for access to required information. The staff consists mainly of subject specialists with many of the traditional functions of acquiring and cataloging of published literature achieved through commercial and network services. A central library capability exists to operate certain basic instructional support functions, provide document delivery services from the remote storage and central collections, and maintain communication and coordination among local information services and the regional, national, and international agencies relied upon for information access and retrieval.

Option Four

Campus coordination of the production, dissemination, and use of scholarly and administrative information is centralized in a highly automated Academic Information Center. University planning councils advise the Center, which has responsibility for policy making, research, operations, funding, and strategic planning for all aspects of academic information use including instruction, research, personnel, financial, curriculum, and student records. Traditional functions included within the Center are computer, library, telecommunications, publishing, and media services.

There is a university vice president in charge of the information function. Information services are equipment-based and highly interactive, with users effectively designing information strategies to solve their research and instructional problems. The primary mode of operation is end user searching of databases without personal assistance. Center staff are largely technical and managerial specialists with a few general purpose information staff. Document storage and bibliographic control functions are maintained by national agencies. Access and delivery services are coordinated by the Academic Information Center.

THE NEED FOR NEW SCENARIOS

These scenarios have been used by OMS for six years in many kinds of projects, including the Leadership Development Program and other strategic planning consulting efforts. Depending on the circumstances, they have been rewritten using the same formula for a computing center, a library network, and a state-wide consortium of libraries. They have also been used in many of the assisted self-study programs, such as the Public Services Review and the Collection Analysis Project, and in workshops that focus on managing change. These scenarios provide a means of opening library staff to the possibilities inherent in those two key concepts—vision and a proactive stance.

Between 1985 and 1987, the results of the scenario assessment activity were analyzed for a number of different OMS projects, including two Management Institutes for ARL Directors, an Advanced Library Management Skills Institute, a Public Services Review Project, and two Leadership Development Programs. A pattern emerged when the assessments of each group for likelihood were plotted against their assessments of the desirability for each of the four scenarios.

Assessments of Scenarios

It is our perception that these assessments have changed. The responses of groups with which OMS has worked over the last two years varies from those in Figure 1. Option One has become both much less likely and much less desirable. Library staff believe they have passed this option by now. Option Two remains as likely, but is seen as less desirable. It does not appear to be enough of a challenge. Option Three seems to be holding its position, and Option Four is still relatively unlikely, but slightly more desirable. Options Three and Four are seen as requiring major changes in the structure of higher education. The assessment of these two options is generally based on the degree to which a group perceives movement in this direction at the local university.

This year, OMS will drop Option One and create a new option for discussion of library futures. It is based on current and emerging technology, discussion with library staff and administrators, and readings from a variety of disciplines. As with the other options, this is not to be construed as our view of the future of academic and research libraries, but one possible future based upon what is known today.

New Option Four

The library has become a gateway to information and information resources and is fully integrated into the teaching and research functions of the university. An infrastructure of technology, facilities, and personal assistance accommodates and supports a wide variety of information gathering behaviors to meet the needs of users whose purpose, subject knowledge, and research sophistication varies widely. The book collections of the library remain physically accessible, but, along with interlibrary loan requests, most materials are requested from and delivered to patrons at service points and offices on the campus.

The core of patron activity is in the information center, a large open access building that houses multi-use computer workstations, study areas, and a service point for document delivery and personal assistance. The center provides access to local and national bibliographic and information databases, most free of charge, but some with fees for use. Users may also prepare texts, send messages, and complete self-paced learning modules using the center's worksta-

Figure 1

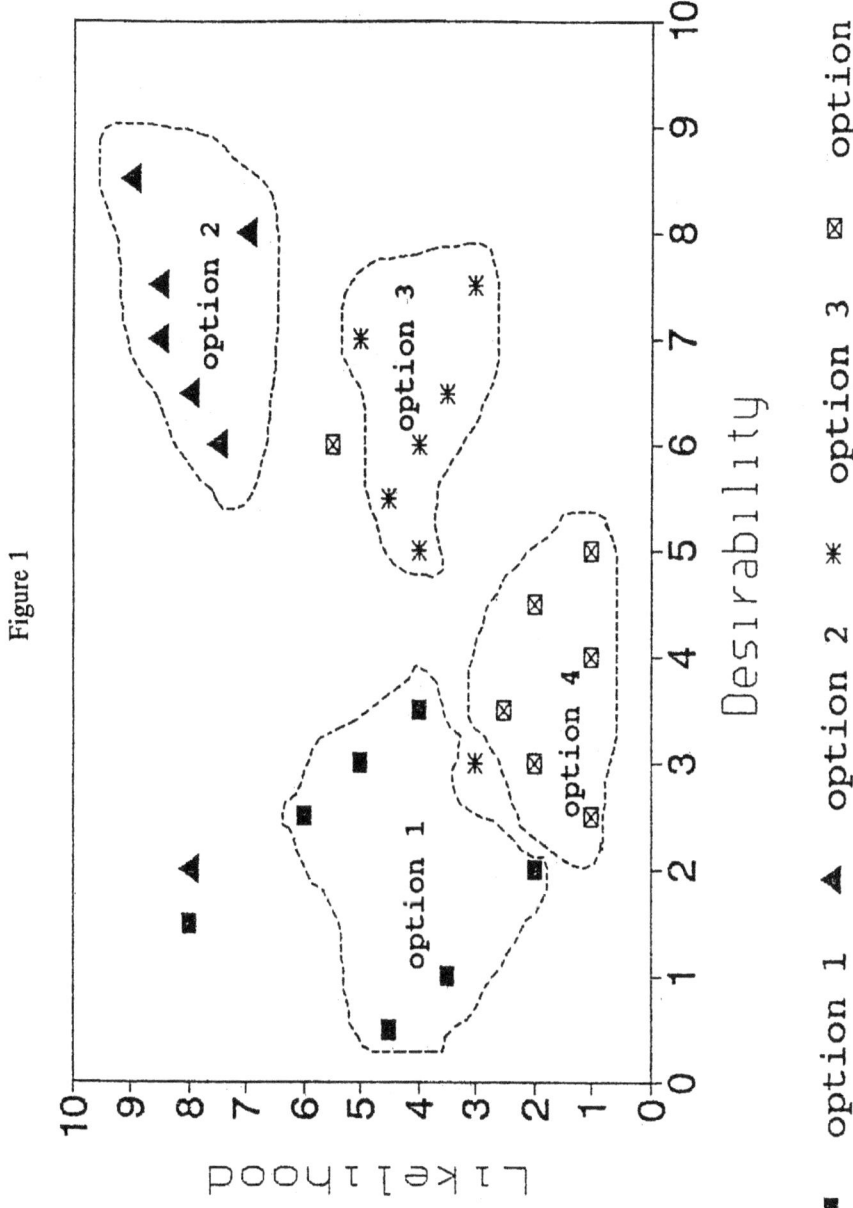

tions. In-depth subject assistance is available at discipline-oriented service clusters distributed around campus. Users at the information center may request assistance from the subject specialists through an online message system or a video conferencing station.

The key result areas in this scenario are fundamentally technological and political in nature. There are sophisticated national and local systems assumed by the information center scenario. Academic and research libraries must continue to play an active role in the development of a national network to facilitate broad access to information. The local systems will require a level of technical support not currently resident in most libraries. A focus on access through resource sharing and other cooperative programs will have to become a reality. The development of an information center must be seen on campus as a partnership between the library, the faculty, the computing center and the university administration.

PREPARING FOR THE FUTURE

Academic and research libraries face new issues in the 1990's that must be addressed in such a way that the libraries can position themselves strategically for the 21st century. Expectations and demands of researchers are changing as patterns of scholarly communication change in response to technological innovation and the information explosion. Many academic and research library buildings are reaching capacity with no new money for growth. Decisions about how to allocate space for materials, service points, and staff will have to be different in an age where there is virtually no money or campus space for new buildings. An increasingly culturally diverse society coupled with reforms contemplated in higher education will have an impact on the kinds of library services and programs needed to support undergraduate education.

There are many different approaches to creating a strategic orientation in preparation for a substantively different future. The "great person" approach places the burden on the shoulders of the leader who can compel others through vision and commitment to follow in new directions. Similarly, an organization can bring in a consultant or group of consultants and accept their expertise in charting a future. And, of course, the future will happen even if no one tries to do anything to influence its course.

It is our belief that the best approach is self-directed and process-oriented. The OMS Leadership Development Program and the strategic planning process described here provides several benefits to a library beyond the creation of a future. It builds a shared perception of the current situation and an opportunity for broad education of the staff regarding trends and innovations. It creates a sense of excitement, ownership, and commitment for the difficult choices that will have to follow in the years to come. There are many opportunities for staff development and training in data gathering, the use of analytical techniques, and group development.

Most important, the LDP process is an exercise in possibility and flexibility. What academic and research libraries will need most as they face an unknowable future is staff who can dream, who have a vision of what they want libraries to be, and who believe they can and should try to create that future. Strategic planning is more than a process or a structure; it is also "an attitude, a way of life."[6] It is an approach that insists on knowing where you want to go, so that you can exploit today's opportunities in order to build a better tomorrow.

REFERENCES

1. Pfeiffer, J.W., Goodstein, L.D., and Nolan, T.M. *Shaping Strategic Planning*. Glenview, IL: Scott, Foresman and Co., 1989.
2. Ackoff, R., Finnel, E.V., and Gharajedaghi, J. *A Guide to Controlling Your Corporate Future*. New York: Wiley, 1984.
3. Ohmae, Kenichi. *The Mind of the Strategist*. New York: McGraw-Hill, 1982.
4. Rockart, J.F. "Chief Executives Define Their Own Data Needs," *Harvard Business Review* 57 (1979): 81-92.
5. Matheson, N.W. and J.A.D. Cooper. "Academic Information in the Academic Health Sciences Center: Roles for the Librarian in Information Management," *Journal of Medical Education* (October 1982, pt.2): 23-25.
6. Steiner, George. *Strategic Planning*. New York: Free Press, 1979.

Performance Measures: A Tool for Planning Resource Allocations

Patricia M. Kelley

SUMMARY. This article introduces the reader to the concept of performance measures, data that indicates to managers how efficiently or effectively or satisfactorily the library serves its clientele. How performance measures differ from current data collection practice, why performance measures are needed and how a measurement program can fold into a library's planning process are emphasized. A short case study demonstrates the author's main points.

INTRODUCTION

"Quality" and "productivity" are business buzzwords that Tom Peters and Lee Iacocca have brought to the discourse of organizations. Academic libraries are not exempt from this conversation, but we must develop a vocabulary that will govern our discussions. The developing concepts of performance measures provide just such a vocabulary.

At the outset, we must begin with words—the data the library collects. What do the data say about the quality of service our faculty and students receive? Do they tell us whether faculty and students find the books and journals they need? Do the data help us analyze the adequacy of facilities? How well do the data support our efforts to reallocate resources effectively or justify requests for additional funding?

As these questions might suggest, most of the management data

---

Patricia M. Kelley is Assistant University Librarian for Programs and Service at George Washington University, Washington, DC.

© 1991 by The Haworth Press, Inc. All rights reserved.

we collect routinely describe our resources and what we do with them. For example, we know how many books and journals we buy, how many hours the library is open, and what proportions of the budget we spend on staff, materials, equipment, and so forth. This information reflects resource allocations, but tells us little about quality. In comparison, when we collect data on specific types of reference transactions, conduct surveys of users, or analyze our collections we have indicators of quality. These surveys are costly or time consuming, for staff and users, so we conduct them infrequently. The data generated over time are rarely comparable because we change the studies. As a result, they do little to help us assess the impact of our decisions. Moreover, in the past we counted our resources and made assumptions about the quality of our libraries on the basis of these statistics. In today's consumer-oriented economy, where the provider is held accountable for meeting consumers' needs, a count of our resources is not enough. We need to know how effective our resource allocations have been in achieving our institutional goals and meeting users' needs.

The need for systematic assessment of the library's performance is becoming critical as our resources are stabilizing or shrinking at the same time that we are supporting changing curricula, rising costs for materials, changing demographics of both workforce and user populations, and rapidly changing technologies that offer new options in development of collections and services. In this age of online information and resource sharing, as emphasis shifts in more libraries from ownership to access, the book count tells us less than it did in earlier years about the quality of our collections or their usefulness for research. Use of collections and visits to the library occur in many ways now, including remote access, so circulation counts and tallies of people entering the building are less descriptive measures of library use than they were in the past. We have more and more choices to make about the kinds of collections we develop, the users' needs to which we give priority, and how we deliver services. And we are doing this in an era when higher education is feeling the pressure to explain its high costs, control tuition hikes, and demonstrate the quality of its work.[1] As one very expensive component of the institution, the need for the library to demonstrate efficiency, effectiveness and user satisfaction is very high. Our ability to keep or increase our share of the economic pie may depend on our skill in demonstrating how well we use the resources provided. As a result, it is imperative that we incorporate performance measurement into our management routines.

WHAT ARE PERFORMANCE MEASURES?

Performance measures serve as the vocabulary that structures our communication. Also called output measures, performance measures are "[counts] and combinations of counts which enable a library to assess the degree to which a program meets its objectives. . . ."[2] They objectively describe how quickly, how accurately, and under what conditions specific activities are accomplished or certain effects are achieved. There are many examples of performance measures, including: numbers of reference transactions, ratio of successful to unsuccessful patron searches for books, and user satisfaction. Such measures provide objective data that we can use to direct resources to meet selected goals and, used retrospectively, to evaluate our success in reaching our objectives. Because goals are specific to the institution, or to each library within the same university, and because performance measures relate to goals, performance data are not useful for comparison across libraries.

Performance measures can be used to assess and evaluate several aspects of library operations within a given library. They typically focus on efficiency of activities when our chief concern is productivity and on effectiveness when our concern is users' needs. For planning purposes, the two often go hand-in-hand; that is, efficient operations usually benefit the user. Only to the extent that he wants to avoid higher tuition rates does a user care whether the library's operations are efficient. The user judges the performance according to how well the library provides materials or services at the time of need. Moreover, he has some expectations about ease of library use or manner of library service. As a result, user satisfaction constitutes a third dimension of measurement.

As an example, interlibrary loan can be used to demonstrate different views of the same activity. A measure of the efficiency of the operation would be indicated by the number of requests processed per employee combined with the rate of success in obtaining items from the first institution polled. If both of those are high, then the activity is judged to be efficient because the data demonstrate that processing of requests is fast and accurate. But if the volume of work is so large that requests are backlogged waiting to be processed, users of the service will find it to be ineffective because it fails to provide the materials at the time of need. The activity may still be highly efficient, but not effective. Furthermore, even if the service is efficient and effective, but users feel poorly served because the staff is unpleasant or the procedures are burdensome to the requestor, then the library's performance is still judged to be poor because users are dissatisfied. All three measures — efficiency, effectiveness, and user satisfaction — are valid bases for evaluation, but they measure different aspects of performance.

MEASURING LIBRARY PERFORMANCE

Performance measures can be applied to units within a library or to the library as a whole. For example, the effectiveness of a check-in procedure may be measured by determining the average time that elapses between receipt of journal issues and their arrival in the pre-shelving area in the periodicals room. Or the library's effectiveness in providing journal literature to its faculty and students may be measured by determining how often library users find desired journal articles in the library. The first example measures one activity, while the second measures the effectiveness of a combination of several, including selection, check-in and binding, shelving and security.

Measures are not standards. A measure provides objective descriptive data; a standard defines a desired level of performance. To be sure, we evaluate our performance by comparing the data we collect through performance measurement to the standards we have established. If we study, for instance, the average lag time between submission of interlibrary loan requests by patrons and the library's transmission of those requests to potential lenders, we may find that we have an average turnaround time of one week. The turnaround time is our performance measure that offers an objective description of the situation. If we state that average turnaround time for processing interlibrary loan requests should be two days, then we are stating a standard. The measures are objective, while standards are subjective. The library administrator's challenge in a consumer-oriented environment is to define a reasonable standard. While performance measures can be used to demonstrate how often the library meets specific needs, the judgement that such performance is effective is a subjective one. Since we are unlikely to meet all users' needs all of the time, realistic performance standards provide a framework for evaluating the objective data we collect through performance measures.

To be used effectively as management tools, performance measures need to be repeated periodically so that they can be used to document and assess change. While one study provides a snapshot of the library's level of performance at a single point in time, the repetition of data collection at intervals works like time-lapse photography to show the evolution that occurs over time as a result of changes in formats of collections, service policies or procedures, staffing levels, and so forth, as well as changing expectations among library users. This was not done in the past because data collection for performance measures requires deliberate staff effort and frequently requires users' cooperation. Much of the time we apply our professional judgement to information collected informally through interactions with users and through observation. While such impressionistic information may have been sufficient for planning during periods of expanding resources, it is less dependable in the current environment.

Numerous efforts have been made over the past fifteen years to develop appropriate methods of analysis for academic and research libraries.[3] Through our professional literature, we can identify a number of types of studies that provide useful data on library performance. The staff effort required varies considerably, depending on the level of specificity desired and degree of error allowed. To take one example, consider methods of studying materials availability. In materials availability studies, we may ask library users to list every book they try to find in the library on a particular visit to the library and, for each book, to note whether or not they are successful. Following one method of analysis, within a very short time period a staff member also tries to find each book and notes whether the patron copied the call number correctly, whether the library owns each one, whether it was on the shelf, whether it was checked out, etc. Such a study requires considerable staff effort and users' cooperation, but can yield detailed information about the reasons for users' failures to obtain materials from the library.[4] At the other extreme, another method of analysis simply compares the number of successful searches by library users and the number of unsuccessful searches.[5] If that ratio is acceptable to the planners, or if the likely reasons for users' failures are obvious, there is no reason to collect detailed information about the causes of failure. Or, a library might perform both types of studies by administering the comprehensive study to establish baseline data, and then use the less detailed study to monitor the overall success rate from year to year. The comprehensive study could be repeated if a significant change in users' failure rate occurs or if a significant procedural, policy, or economic change is likely to affect users' ability to locate materials. Regardless of the method employed in gathering data, interpretation of the information provided by performance measures requires no less professional judgement than we have exercised in the past. The advantage is in the objectivity of the information we are assessing when we use data gathered systematically through the application of performance measures.

LINKING PERFORMANCE MEASURES TO THE PLANNING PROCESS

Performance measures may be most useful in the planning and evaluation stages of the planning process because they indicate how well we are achieving our objectives. Depending upon the type of planning process used, the collection of performance data may even be specified in the plan.

Consider, for example, the library that follows a strategic planning model, a process that has become quite popular among institutions that are engaged in planning for change. Using this model, the written plan includes only organizational goals that direct library-wide resources to meet selected challenges, such as implementation of an integrated computer system or creation of a new service. Goals and objectives for ongoing operations do not appear in this plan. The decision to implement a systematic program of performance measurement in a library probably will be a strategic goal in its own right because initiation of this program will require a staff education program, allocation of significant staff time and effort and, perhaps, funds. Continuation of the program will also require staff time and effort, but at a maintenance level. Therefore, once the program is established it probably will no longer be visible in the strategic plan. The data from performance measures, however, become an important part of the strategic planning process, and the systematic collection of data must continue as part of library operations. For example, in the Gelman Library of George Washington University, the strategic plans for 1987 and 1988 reflected our decision to implement performance measures pertaining to the accessibility of collections and services. The plan for 1987 included the staff education component and planning for data collection, while the 1988 plan called for data collection and analysis. While we will repeat the studies at regular intervals in future years, they will be considered ongoing library operations. In other words, although they will become an important component of departmental and divisional operational plans, they are unlikely to be mentioned in the strategic plan. The data that continue to be collected, however, feed into the strategic planning process because it is one source of objective information that we can use in assessing our ability to meet the near future needs of our user community. When the strategic plan calls for significant changes in services, facilities or collections, such goals will be based in part on the performance data from these ongoing studies.

Elsewhere, libraries that use more comprehensive planning methods are more likely to include data collection and analysis as explicit goals in written plans. Although the initial implementation effort for a performance measurement program requires the greatest time and effort, even ongoing data collection requires staff effort and a significant amount of time on the part of the coordinator. Inevitably, compiling and analyzing the data require considerable effort on an ongoing basis.

Elements of a Planning Process

No matter what planning model is used, the elements of planning are similar. We collect information about our environment, and analyze the information to determine whether or not it indicates a need to adapt operations to meet changing needs. Then we decide what changes to make, and how to make them. After evaluating these changes, we again examine the environment, and the cycle continues. Performance measures help us analyze our environment, while changes in performance data help evaluate our success in effecting change. Both the snapshot provided by a single study and the pictures of change that emerge from repetitions of the study provide useful planning information.

If resources were limitless, identifying growing demands and allocating the resources to fulfill them would be a simple process. If the need for one type of service or facility automatically replaced the need for another, then we could simply reallocate resources from the old to the new. If there were just one way to meet each goal or a universal agreement on what the library's goals should be, then solutions would be self-evident. Unfortunately, none of those scenarios represents reality. Resources are finite, perhaps shrinking. The types of services and facilities and the areas of necessary collection development that are needed or strongly desired by our users tend to multiply. Even when needs for different facilities or services evolve, there is a period of overlap when we must deal with demands for both the old and the new. We are working in an age of rapid expansion in publication and information, compounded by ever increasing choices of technologies for delivery of information. In short, we have many choices to make. Using performance data to describe objectively the extent to which we fulfill the myriad demands on our resources, we can evaluate how well the choices we made achieved our goals.

Relationship Between Goals and Performance Measures

The first step in using performance measures in the planning process is to examine planning goals to decide how we will know when each goal has been achieved. For example, where our faculty have the choice of many libraries to use in conducting their research, we may have a goal of increasing the faculty members' use of their own library. In other words, we want the faculty to have confidence that they can meet most of their research needs through the collections and services (including interlibrary loan, full-text databases, etc.) of their home library. If this library regularly collects performance data, it will know the turnaround time on interlibrary loan and other document delivery services, the find rate for books and periodicals in its own collections, as well as some survey data indicating what collections and services faculty use and how often. It may even have survey data indicating what other libraries the faculty use and how often. To meet its goal, the library may do a number of things to increase faculty awareness of its collections and services, add staff to key areas in an effort to make improvements, and so forth. The performance data would indicate whether speed of service had improved, whether patterns of use of targeted services had changed, and whether faculty use of the home library and other libraries had changed.

Relationship of Resource Allocations and Performance Measures

The resources to achieve goals need to come from reallocations within the library or new resources. If a goal is achieved through reallocation, then performance measures can help in assessing the impact on the operations that "contributed" resources. For example, use data may indicate that little use is made of one service in the evening, so staff time is reallocated to an activity that is experiencing growing demand. While there will be grumbling and complaints from people who were accustomed to evening service at that service point, the library is in a particularly good position to demonstrate the wisdom of its decision if the use data have been collected as a part of routine data collection. A one-time study simply lacks the credibility of systematically collected data.

When a goal can be accomplished only through allocation of new resources or through reallocations that will be painful to the users, then objective data are even more essential. Our responses to skyrocketing serials prices in recent years provide good examples of that. Libraries have met the challenge through a combination of additional funding (some new, some reallocated) and cancellation of subscriptions. Those who have data on the use of journals by subject area, if not by title, have been in a better position to defend their decisions on retention or cancellation than have libraries that depend on professional judgement alone. After the fact, interlibrary loan and other document delivery data as well as data collected in materials availability studies help assess the initial decisions. This is just one example of the many trade-offs we make in planning distribution of staff, equipment and other resources. When confronted with the need to make choices, we often wish we had reliable information. While performance measures seldom provide conclusive data, they do provide good information for planning and evaluating library activities. They serve as a common language for understanding the choices we have and the effects of the choices we make.

IMPLEMENTING PERFORMANCE MEASURES

Adoption of performance measures as planning tools depends on two critical conditions. First, administrators and managers throughout the library need to recognize that collection of accurate performance data is an essential, ongoing management function. Just as we routinely count the number of books we add to the collection, so we routinely need to count the number of people waiting in lines at our service desks and find out whether our user community is satisfied with our performance. Regardless of whether we are counting inputs or performances, we simply collect data that describe the situation so that we can make choices that are based on objective information when we allocate space, staff, equipment and so forth. Unless managers at all levels appreciate the value of performance data for operational assessment, performance measures will be meaningless exercises.

The second condition is staff cooperation, preferably staff enthusiasm. While staff members routinely collect statistics about their daily work, they receive little reward for doing so. Recording these statistics is a requirement, perhaps a nuisance, but the staff rarely sees the data used in planning. Performance measures require more data collection and more conscious effort than do input measures, particularly when a measure requires the cooperation of library users. Implementing performance measures will divert some effort from production and service activities and may elicit negative information. In order to cooperate, the staff need to feel that the effort and time invested in data collection are well spent.

Adoption of performance measures as management tools requires a close partnership among administrators, mid-level managers, and front-line staff because collection and analysis of data require effort at all levels. The success of this joint endeavor, like successful partnerships anywhere, depends upon a shared belief that all partners contribute to and all benefit from pursuit of shared goals. Since most libraries are hierarchical organizations, the partnership is unequal in many respects. Moreover, performance measures are intended to be used to identify problems and document needs as well as to confirm perceptions and document successes. Performance measures are intended to be used for resource allocation. So, not only are the partners unequal, but some purposes can be viewed as threatening. Together, those conditions can create barriers to implementation of performance measures.

Overcoming the barriers is a continual process, in which the first and most difficult step is to understand the factors within the organization that support as well as those that threaten implementation of performance measurement. The most difficult concepts that have to be understood are: the difference between inputs and performances; the relationship between performance measures and professional judgement in decision making; and the fact that the organization, not the individual, is the subject of study. It is essential that everyone understand what performance measures are and how they will be used. More important, key individuals need to see the link between the data that will be collected and the library's goals and planning process.

A Case Study

The process of adopting performance measures as management tools will vary among institutions, depending on the management relationships and corporate culture within the individual organization. However, a brief case study of the implementation of a performance measures program in George Washington University's Gelman Library demonstrates one useful approach. Gelman Library is the main library on campus.

The library's Policy and Planning Group, composed of the three administrators and three members elected by the librarians and graded staff, has primary responsibility for library-wide planning efforts, including development and management of the strategic plan. In the mid 1980's this planning group, in cooperation with librarians and other management staff, made the conscious decision to evaluate the quality of library activities. We assigned priorities to various areas of concern, including accessibility of collections and services, quality of collections, and sufficiency of user space. Recognizing that we could not take on all concerns at once, the planning group assigned each area to a planning year and developed a model for implementation of measurement and assessment. Ours is a two-year model in which we spend the first year developing the measures we will use and the second year applying and analyzing the measures. For example, development of performance measures concerning accessibility of collections and services was assigned to the 1987/88 and 1988/89 academic years, collection quality to 1988/89 and 1989/90. During the spring and summer of 1987 we initiated an education program to teach ourselves (administrators and heads of departments and units within the library) about performance measures through reading and discussion. With the help of a consultant, the Policy and Planning Group and department heads held a one-day retreat to clarify our understanding of performance measures and learn some very basic statistical concepts and research methods.

Then we began to plan the data collection. After coming to a mutual understanding of what we meant by accessibility, the heads of service departments worked with their staff members to define departmental information needs. As expected, the needs are similar throughout the library. All departments need to know what patron groups they serve at various times of the day, week, and semester. We need to determine if there are predictable patterns to demand so that we can do a better job of staffing. And we want to check our perceptions about the use patterns of service-dependent equipment (such as catalog terminals, photocopy machines, microform readers, etc.). In addition, we need to know whether users find the materials they seek in the collection and how well we provide materials we need to acquire elsewhere. Except for user satisfaction, all identified information needs could be met reasonably well through three types of studies: scheduled observations, tallies made at service desks, and additional notations on existing work forms. While the extra tallies and notations became the responsibility of service staff, supplemental student staff were hired and supervised by administration to conduct the observations. Data collected at service desks were sent to administration for the time-consuming compilation tasks.

What did we gain from these efforts? Some of our assumptions about use patterns were confirmed, and with confidence based on hard data we were able to reduce hours of service at one desk and implement new and somewhat controversial practices in another service area. Much to our relief, we found that some of our impressions were wrong, particularly some assumptions we had made about unmet demand for equipment that supports use of collections. We shifted staffing allocations among functions within departments, and feel that we are already seeing positive benefits from those adjustments. Finally, we identified some improvements we will want to make when finances permit and some improvements that need to become a higher priority than we had previously assumed.

To the best of our ability, we continue that pattern of planning and implementation as we adopt other measures. In other words, we try to ensure that the data we collect will be considered useful at many levels of the organization, and we share the burden of the additional data collection.

The process of thinking about performance measures and deciding what data to collect is very enlightening. Once staff members begin thinking in terms of what they wish they could know about the use of their services, they become very alert to patterns of user behavior and the cause-and-effect relationships between library behavior and user behavior. With data to support perceptions, department heads seem to speak more confidently about operational problems and changes. They appear to be more conscious of statistics and comparisons of activity levels at different points in time.

For a number of reasons, Gelman Library's staff members are particularly willing to use performance measures. Our library, located on an urban downtown campus, is open to the public and is used heavily by students from other universities and by employees of firms and government agencies. As a result, library staff members are attuned to the competing demands of different user groups and receptive to studies that help document and analyze patterns of those demands. We know that our perceptions of our own faculty and students' needs are skewed by the demands we feel from unaffiliated researchers. That understanding gives us a vested interest in formal study of our activities that may be difficult to achieve in more traditional academic settings. Moreover, organizational assessment based on a questionnaire administered annually among the staff was in place for a few years before we introduced performance measures. As a result, the concept of organizational measurement and assessment was well established before we attempted to apply performance measures to particular activities within the organization. Those circumstances are not prerequisites for success; rather, they are examples of factors within one library that support the use of performance measures in planning. This library also has negative factors that other libraries would not have, the chief one being the sizable population of unaffiliated users who do not have a vested interest in cooperating during library studies. The need to separate their expressed needs from the needs of primary user groups complicates data collection and raises the level of effort and cost. In every library there are conditions that support the use of performance measures as well as conditions that undermine their use.

Identifying the opportunities and threats before attempting to implement a program of measurement can help maximize the supporting forces and minimize the effects of negative factors.

CONCLUSION

Performance measures are not a new concept, though they have not been used systematically in academic library planning in the past. In the current political and economic climate, when legislatures, parents, students and the business world are questioning whether higher education is worth its high price tag, we have a much stronger need to engage in objective discussion about the library's usefulness and effectiveness. Now we find that our users are assertive consumers whose needs are increasingly diverse and that, though our resources are finite, we enjoy rapidly expanding options for meeting the ever changing and widely differing users' needs. Making rational and acceptable choices requires much more open dialog than it did in the past. To ensure clarity, we need to use a language that can be understood by librarians and university administrators. Performance measures provide us the vocabulary for conducting the dialog, for defining users' needs, describing the library's performance in terms of efficiency, effectiveness and user satisfaction, and planning to meet future challenges. A growing body of literature offers performance measures we can use confidently as tools for managing the present and shaping our future.

NOTES

1. States' efforts to ensure accountability of colleges and universities for the quality of education is summarized in Goldie Blumenstyk, "Diversity Is Keynote of States' Efforts to Assess Students' Learning," *Chronicle of Higher Education*, 35 (July 20, 1988): A17, A25-26.
2. Mary Jo Lynch, ed., *Library Data Collection Handbook* (Chicago: American Library Association, 1981), 178.
3. An excellent summary of research trends in the area of performance measures and a bibliography of useful literature will appear in Nancy Van House, Beth Weil, and Charles R. McClure, *Output Measures for Academic Libraries: A Practical Handbook* (Chicago: American Library Association, 1990).

4. Two useful guides to performing this type of study include "Measurement of Availability Using Patron Requests and Branching Theory" in *Objective Performance Measures for Academic and Research Libraries*, Paul B. Kantor (Washington, DC: Association of Research Libraries, 1984), 43-56; Rita Hoyt Smith and Warner Granade, "User and Library Failures in an Undergraduate Library," *College and Research Libraries* 39 (November 1978), 467-473.

5. An example of this type of study is provided in Douglas Zweizig and Eleanor Jo Rodger, *Output Measures for Public Libraries* (Chicago: American Library Association, 1982), 51-55.

Creating Your Library's Future Through Effective Strategic Planning

Brice G. Hobrock

SUMMARY. The uncertain political, economic, and social environments faced by libraries of all types in the 1990's can be anticipated through the use of effective strategic planning. Strategic planning, a planning philosophy that links programs to the external environment, is well-suited to libraries where scarce resources must be concentrated in areas that anticipate the future and respond to external and highly-competitive conditions. Strategic planning is defined and is compared to other planning methodologies used by libraries. Conditions necessitating strategic planning are reviewed and a typical strategic planning methodology is suggested. As effective strategic planning must ultimately be linked to resources, budgetary factors are discussed. Overall, the paper encourages library managers to think and act strategically.

INTRODUCTION

Clearly, strategic planning offers the best opportunity for library managers to create an effective future for the library organization. Considering the changing and uncertain political, financial, and social environments expected in the 1990's, anticipating and planning for the library's future is essential. Libraries are not known for comprehensive or futuristic planning and library managers are not consistently prepared to lead necessary planning efforts. Nevertheless, in the 1990's all successful libraries and library directors must adopt planning methodologies that allow the library to compete for scarce resources. "Plan or be planned for"[1] and "instead of worrying

---

Brice G. Hobrock is Professor and Dean of Libraries at Kansas State University, Manhattan, KS.

© 1991 by The Haworth Press, Inc. All rights reserved.

about the future, let us labor to create it,"[2] are operative messages for the 1990's. Consequently, the principles and processes of strategic planning are presented here as the means by which library managers at all levels can create and control the library's future.

Strategic planning is ideally suited for the unpredictable futures that libraries face. During the late 1980's, libraries of all types faced erosion of financial resources, the continued explosion of published information, and the appearance of new technologies. No abatement in the occurrence of such challenges is expected in the next decade. The Association of Research Libraries[3] reported that the average cost of purchased serials rose by 31 percent between 1986 and 1988. The *Chronicle of Higher Education*[4] reported that the average cost of science journals purchased by research libraries in the U.S. and Canada rose 44 percent between 1986 and 1989. And, during the period, 1978 to 1988, 29,621 new science journals were created. How does a library plan future programs and budgets in such an environment? Is bigger always better, and can we expect the continued addition of new resources? What choices will have to be made in the 1990's when libraries cannot afford adequate collections and comprehensive services? The assertion here, thus, is that only strategic planning can prepare the library to deal with such a future.

Consequently, this discussion defines strategic planning and compares it with other planning methodologies that have been and may still be in use in libraries. The paper continues by outlining conditions expected in the 1990's that will make strategic planning essential. A systematic strategic planning methodology is next outlined for libraries followed by resource acquisition guidelines. Finally, concluding comments emphasize the overall consequences and importance of strategic planning for libraries.

PLANNING TYPOLOGIES: STRATEGIC PLANNING DEFINED AND COMPARED

In the author's view, "to make no plan is to accept a future that external events and others decide for us." It is a unique human characteristic to wonder about the future and what it will bring.

Man's religious, governmental and social institutions inherently reflect a wish to control the present and create the future. Throughout man's history, the evidence of his activities show that organized planning was used. Clearly, from the evidence provided by ruins and artifacts of ancient civilizations, organized planning controlled construction, farming, and other rituals of daily life. Based upon knowledge of his environment, such as the angle of the sun and the phases of the moon, man made choices for the future based on that knowledge. Also, based upon knowledge and available information, each person in modern society plans as far into the future as possible. Consequently, we actually do informal strategic planning, making choices, based on knowledge of the environment, without being aware of it.

Unfortunately, there has been too little attention paid to planning methodologies as essential skills for library managers. Generally, there is limited formalized training in basic MLS professional programs because library managers are not identified until librarians gain considerable experience. As librarians move from line to management positions, efforts are not often made to acquire formal planning skills. Library managers, consequently, need to understand the basic differences between traditional and strategic planning and seek necessary skills. Strategic planning is defined here and compared to several traditional planning methodologies used in libraries since 1945.

Strategic Planning Defined

Definitions of strategic planning abound. There is no universally-accepted single and succinct definition. Fundamentally, however, strategic planning may be best defined as both an intellectual exercise and a process that concentrates resources[5] in areas that anticipate the future. Bryson[6] defines "strategic planning as a disciplined effort to produce fundamental decisions and actions that shape and guide what an organization is, what it does, and why it does it." Nevertheless, strategic planning is less a set of formalized procedures than a mindset, a way of thinking about the future. The strategic thinker contemplates the future, and determines and implements those actions that will bring the greatest return from available resources. More importantly, strategic thinking conditions managers to define the most basic characteristics of the organization and to think in terms of what is most important to immediate and medium-range futures. Moreover, strategic planning is ideally applied in resource-poor (think libraries) organizations where choices must be made about which services best respond to future demands.

Keller[7] states that there are "six features that distinguish strategic planning from such predecessors as systems analysis, incrementalism, management science, long-range planning, and doing what you have always done."

Strategic planning is active rather than passive. It assumes that the planners will take positive steps to anticipate opportunities and threats and actually shape the future.

It looks outward rather than inward. External factors increasingly have a greater effect on the organizational future than internal traditions and policies.

It is competitive. Libraries must realize that benevolent declarations that the library is "the heart of the community (university)" no longer apply when resources are scarce. An organization with a strategic plan is positioned to compete effectively in a hostile, competitive environment.

Strategic planning focuses on decisions, rather than plans, goals, analyses, or forecasts. The strategic thinker and planner determines what shall be done to best utilize available resources to meet future opportunities and demands.

It is participatory and tolerant of controversy. There need not be a consensus among decision-makers. However, as Moran[8] points out, top managers must reserve the power to make resource allocations and implementation decisions. Nevertheless, it is important to permit all rational and irrational input, and political maneuvering by participants.

Finally, strategic planning concentrates on the fate of the library. It assumes that long-term survival and vitality of the organization is most important. It preserves traditions but places organizational survival above sacred cows. How many businesses, universities and libraries will survive the 1990's as viable organizations? The list of business organizations and colleges that cease operations grows because they did not anticipate the future environment. How many libraries will remain as book warehouses, bypassed through failure to anticipate the role and importance of broad-based electronic access and information technology?

Other Methodologies Compared

The above characteristics define strategic planning and typical procedures for strategic planning are reviewed below. However, several other conventional planning methodologies should be described to establish essential differences with strategic planning. Long-range planning, management science, incrementalism and Planning, Programming and Budgeting (PPB) are reviewed here as important historical precursors of strategic planning.

Conventional planning in libraries is often limited to generic short- and long-range plans. Long-range planning sets objectives, develops strategies and programs for implementation and may involve management data and budget. However, time-based approaches have limited utility in a rapidly-changing world. Bryson[9] indicates that although long-range planning is often used synonymously in some organizations with strategic planning, long-range planning lacks a consistent philosophy and does not consider the effects of the future environment. Long-range plans assume that current trends will continue into the future. Moran states that "strategic planners feel that long-range plans will almost always fail because environmental conditions change rapidly and plans become obsolete." "Strategic planners concentrate on short-range and medium-range issues and usually work within a time-frame of three to five years." ". . . strategic plans are . . . continuously updated as the need arises."[10]

Management science believes that systematic data-based management methodologies prevail over day-to-day "make it up as you go" management. The latter has been too commonly state-of-the-art planning in libraries. Although management science had its philosophical beginnings in the late 18th century in France, its American godfather, Frederick Taylor, provided the empirical basis for its applications.[11] Taylor founded time-studies and efficiency engineering and believed that scientific principles would resolve most managerial problems. The modern cousins of Taylor's work include systems analysis, operations research, institutional research, modeling, cost-effectiveness, and management information systems. Advocates of management science believed that diagnosis of a management unit, particularly if supported by mathematical models and data, could reveal weaknesses or assess productivity in relation to available resources. Unfortunately, while such studies provided the means for improvement of individual units of an organization, they lacked the ability to look at the total organization and its future. In some cases, data tended to obscure the realities of the system.

The techniques of management science were used by many large libraries in the 1960's and 1970's but its use is largely discredited today because of the lack of a relationship to the future environment. As libraries implement automated systems with large management report outputs, care must be taken to insure that data-based "management science" data does not overwhelm strategic decision-making.

Incremental planning, the most passive of all formalized planning, is still entrenched in some libraries. Its practice in the 1960's and 1970's was strong enough to hold off inroads by more formalized management science and PPB approaches. Incrementalism assumes that resource acquisition is largely political and that the astute politician will get the bigger piece of the pie. Usually, however, change results "through hundreds of tiny little steps, no one of which is heavy-footed enough to rock the boat."[12] Across-the-board approaches to resource allocation especially play into the incrementalism trap. Incrementalism fails to address organized change, relationships of budget to priorities, evaluation of program effectiveness, and the future environment. Budgetary processes disguised as "program enhancement funding" are often only incrementalism in sheep's clothing. Libraries, who have long enjoyed special status in community, social, and educational arenas, have had much success with incremental approaches. It too often perpetuates, however, the patching of an existing system without looking at problems and the future environment. Consequently, as the environmental factors of the 1990's are considered, incrementalism is less likely to survive.

According to Keller,[13] until PPB appeared in 1961, these two types of planning, management science and incrementalism, had dominated American planning since 1945. PPB linked long-range objectives, programs, and budget requirements and was, thus, a vast improvement over management science, incremental planning and time-based projections. These latter methods do not ordinarily deal with the relationships among objectives, programs, and budget. And, as we will see, PPB provided many of the tools used by today's strategic planner. Some applications of PPB, when linked to environmental analysis, may pass for strategic planning.

PPB is considered to be an important precursor to strategic planning as it developed in a postwar Defense Department environment where limited funds had to be allocated among many programs. PPB was an attempt to integrate policy formulation and decision-making with budget allocation. It also provided the means to bring systematic analysis to bear on the process. According to Schultze,[14] PPB is primarily concerned with the determination of organizational objectives and the selection of programs. It also presumes that program selection decisions will be aided by systematic analysis and objective criteria. Finally, it develops a systematic planning process that strengthens the authority of upper management. Like strategic planning it is primarily a technique of upper management. The similarities and differences between the stepwise processes of PPB and strategic planning will be noted.

The systematic PPB process as outlined by Schultze first establishes goals and objectives for each major operational area of the organization. The second step analyzes output of all programs and operational areas in terms of those goals and objectives.

In the third step, PPB measures total program costs for current programs and estimates costs of those programs several years ahead. In this step, two kinds of costs are considered, (a) future budgetary consequences of current decisions, and (b) costs incurred outside the program by the decision. This latter point, how the current decision affects related programs, is often overlooked if planning takes place at too low a level in the organization. In such a case, managers view their programs and decisions as isolated entities and events. PPB, thus, requires managers to look at the effect that programs and budget decisions have on other areas.

Step four formulates objectives and programs needed beyond the current budget. This "long-range planning" step is effective, however, only if it predicts the expected environment.

A fifth step analyzes the alternatives. It identifies the most effective means for reaching program objectives at least cost. It provides the means to choose, using objective considerations, which programs will give the most cost-effective results. In effect, step five incorporates cost-effective analysis into the overall PPB process. This particular step was probably the most direct reaction to the need to displace incrementalism as a budget practice. It could be "strategic" as it provides some basis for making choices among programs.

Finally, the last step establishes analysis as part of the systematic budget review. The intention is to integrate decision-making and the budget process. It is at this point that resources must be allocated among competing programs based upon information gained in the previous steps. Consideration of objective criteria, i.e., program objectives and their effectiveness and cost, thus, contributes to strategic decision-making. Program analysis and decision-making, therefore, come together with budget at this point.

We will see, subsequently, that many of the characteristics and processes of PPB are carried into the strategic planning process. The major difference is that PPB does not consider the future environment in a formal way. On the other hand, strategic planning efforts often fail if budget is not associated with programs.

A primary distinction outlined here, then, between strategic planning and PPB, management science, long-range planning, and incrementalism is noted in the way that planning methodologies deal with future environmental factors. Of course, few librarians are trained as prognosticators. However, as users and managers of current information, library managers can easily assess political, social, and economic trends that will affect libraries. A summary of easily-predictable environmental events follows.

CONDITIONS THAT FAVOR STRATEGIC PLANNING IN THE 1990's

These are difficult times for library managers. The good old days of the 1960's and 1970's, when the electorate was willing to routinely approve new taxes for buildings and services for its public institutions, were replaced by the tax reductions and growth-based economics of the 1980's. "No new taxes" promises to be the dominant public policy of the 1990's. The majority of privately-supported institutions, dependent upon endowments and fund-raising, cannot help but be affected by tax-related forces, as well. Collectively, the pressures of increasing costs of information, new technologies, a restructured world order, changing demographics, and new expectations for service from users affect all libraries and create new dilemmas.

Improvements in the majority of library services and adaptations to change in the 1990's will likely come from the corpus of the existing organization. It is important, consequently, for the library to recognize trends and conditions that shape a changing and future environment. Keller,[15] Bryson,[16] Radford,[17] and others describe certain underlying conditions and trends that call for careful, futuristic planning. The library manager's ability to analyze current and predictable events is critical.

In the 1990's, there will be increased competition for scarce funds within both public and private sectors. Libraries do not necessarily retain the priorities they once enjoyed. The demands of the environment, social welfare, drug enforcement and treatment, law enforcement and prisons, tax abatement, and restoration of the public infrastructure are all providing intense competition. Public polls indicate that education and libraries all rank below these issues in the public perception. Within higher education, faculty and administrators grow tired of the continuing demands of libraries to build new warehouse libraries and for funding to support the effects of journal cost inflation.

There is increasing communication and interconnection of the world. There is blurring between domestic and international source and publication of information. Research information has become an international commodity. The worldwide nature of communications results in wider involvement and concern about the issues of the day.

Interdependence among public, private, and non-profit institutions grows at a rapid rate. Government is taking less responsibility for its public institutions. And, as competition for public funds increases, public institutions are advised to seek private funding in order to meet basic services. This growing interdependence requires that libraries think and plan strategically. Governmental privatization of information invites the private sector to take a greater, for-profit role in the dissemination of information. As publishing costs rise, non-profit learned societies have transferred traditional journal title publishing to the private for-profit sector.

Change occurs in rapid and unpredictable ways. Libraries too often react as if the world were static rather than dynamic. The world order is being turned completely upside down in early 1990. Dramatic political and social changes in Eastern and Central Europe, the Soviet Union, China, and Central and South America are expected almost daily. This worldwide "perestroika" or restructuring can be expected to continue for many years. How do libraries anticipate the resulting rapid changes in information sources, output, and access that will be necessary to support our users?

Demographics, and hence, library users are changing. The ethnic composition of the United States in the 1990's will become radically different. Immigration and birth rates have already altered the demographics of library users. Afro-American, Asian, Hispanic, and Middle-Eastern user populations are expected to grow to the point where persons of European origin are a minority. English will remain as the dominant language but other languages will become important, as well. Academic libraries, that have done business as usual despite increasing numbers of students from China and other Asian countries, will now be serving new students from Eastern Europe and the Soviet Union. How will libraries anticipate the changes that will be necessary?

Since the publication of "A Nation at Risk,"[18] it has been clear that there is a crisis in American education. Increasingly, the U.S. educational system is criticized here and abroad as being inferior. Poor ACT/SAT scores, poor mathematics performance by students, no knowledge of geography, declining numbers of domestic graduate students, and many other factors are being identified as evidence of a non-competitive educational system. The shortage of qualified faculty and librarians in the 1990's is expected to severely impact higher education and libraries. What role do libraries have in this environment?

U.S. competitiveness in research and technology is steadily declining. Japan, for example, literally dominates electronics and microchip research and technology. As most modern military and consumer goods depend upon technology, the United States may soon fall into dependency on other countries. Libraries play a key role in supporting research and development. How do we prepare to support new initiatives in research that must occur in the 1990's?

Worldwide currency values and financial systems greatly affect cost and output of information. The U.S. dollar was highly valued against currencies of developed nations until early 1985, but dropped in value as the U.S. Government desired to make U.S. products more affordable abroad. While trade deficits have not improved as much as desired, the effect of dollar devaluation on American libraries has been devastating. Devaluation, coupled with the extraordinary growth in European information materials, is limiting the abilities of North American and Third World libraries to acquire needed materials.

Information technology is evolving rapidly. New information technology is causing some of the most dramatic transformations in the storage and retrieval of information since the introduction of printing in the fifteenth century.[19] Electronic and optical formats coupled with the power of the computer are expanding and transforming the libraries of the 1990's. Not only do libraries have to finance the new formats and hardware that this very expensive technology requires, but must deal with the facilities and services that must be provided. Deterioration of collections should be mentioned, finally, as one of the great issues of the coming decade. A strategic dilemma exists about whether a library would choose to preserve information at the cost of foregoing purchase and shelving of new information.

The economic, social, and technological environment for libraries in the 1990's promise to be even more challenging than the decade of the 1980's. Nevertheless, by anticipating the future and applying the principles of strategic thinking and planning, libraries can create effective roles and competitive futures.

PROCEDURES FOR DEVELOPING A STRATEGIC PLAN

Universal strategic plans or strategic planning processes do not exist. Each plan is unique to the organization and depends upon needs. Concomitantly, procedures leading to a successful strategic plan also will vary with the unique characteristics of each organization. There are, however, common procedural elements developed for higher education and business that are applicable to libraries. Keller,[20] Below,[21] Bryson,[22] Melcher,[23] and many others outline procedures that may be adapted to libraries. Eight detailed steps are presented here that can be utilized for library strategic planning. However, some libraries and smaller managerial units may wish to abbreviate the number of formal steps. Considering only four key steps; objectives, environmental factors, strategies, and programs, should suffice in many cases. Budget considerations can be incorporated at the program level.

A detailed formal strategic planning effort, nevertheless, may include all of the following steps.

A first step is to establish the ground rules for the strategic planning effort. In this first step, all participants must be fully informed and committed to the necessity for strategic planning and to the processes to be used in the strategic planning effort. Some useful guidelines are outlined here. (See Bryson[24] for a more detailed account.) Rules for this first step include:

- A strategic planning effort requires that top management be committed to and fully schooled about the process. Otherwise, as the process solicits input from the entire library and proceeds to implementation, there cannot be wholehearted participation from rank and file. Also, as pointed out earlier, implementation depends upon the decision-making and resource allocation responsibilities of management. Management must "champion" and sponsor the process.
- There should next be a strategic planning task force or team appointed to coordinate the effort. Smaller libraries may want to involve only senior staff or the entire staff. Be sure to include or consult paraprofessional staff at some stage of the process.
- It is very important that the entire process be fully defined and methodologies understood by all participants before the process begins. Step one cannot be started without steps two

through eight being known. A realistic time line for completing the steps should be proposed, but should allow flexibility if snags are encountered.
- There must be realistic expectations that a strategic planning process will result in positive outcomes for the library. Realistic financial guidelines must accompany the process document. A strategic plan that cannot be implemented for lack of resources is more damaging than if no plan had been created.
- Sufficient time must be made available for strategic planning. It must become a scheduled activity for participants. Conducting business as usual while doing strategic planning will result in a stressed organization and a less effective plan.
- Reading materials and paperwork should be minimized. Seek clarity and brevity in all information collected. The strategic planning document itself should be brief and formatted for easy reading.
- Establish clear lines of communication and communicate progress at each step. Circulate reports of progress to all stakeholders in the process. Seek ideas from the grassroots. Not all good ideas come from management.

Clarification of the library's mandate or mission is an important second step. The organizational mission determines what the library does and who it serves. It defines organizational purpose and the reason the organization exists. It is a focal point around which all participants can support the planning effort. Also, since libraries provide services to a parent organization, the mission of the parent unit must be recognized as the library mission is defined. If library strategic planning is done in concert with a parent organization, the parent may provide formal guidance in the form of a "charge." The charge provides a framework for planning. The library may also provide a charge to its separate planning units. "Boundaries" are established by this step.

The third step is to conduct an environmental analysis. Sometimes called the "strategic analysis," the activity assesses the internal and external factors that affect the library now and in the predictable future. The environmental analysis, further, becomes the database, the reference point against which strategic issues are identified. It defines the future conditions against which the library must make strategic choices and decisions. The environmental analysis could suitably be defined in terms of both opportunities and threats. While most "futures" outlined above may be interpreted as threats, many could be considered as opportunities to make sweeping changes in the organization.

Resource analysis, a fourth step defined by some planners, will systematically assess strengths and weaknesses of the library as perceived by staff and the user community. Clearly, assessment of the organization cannot be left to management and staff alone. As librarians are purveyors of information services to a clientele, a credible resource analysis could include a user response to this question. An assessment of financial resources and expectations may be included here.

Following analysis of the environment and library assets in steps three and four, the strategic planner will next wish to identify the strategic issues that face the library for the next one to five years. Moran[25] defines a similar step as a reformulation of the library's current goals. Nevertheless, identification of the strategic issues here in this fifth step provides a framework for defining strategies. The strategic issues of the library might also be presented as "themes," or statements of intent concerning future activities. A typical issue or theme might be, "despite hyperinflation of research journals in science, the library intends to provide current science research information, regardless of source, in support of research programs." The strategic issue or "theme" would be followed in the next step by "strategies" which would accomplish the intent of the "theme." Bryson[26] and others speak of establishing a "vision" of the organization at this point. A "vision" is an idealized image of what the library should look like in the future. Since strategic planning involves top management who have a view of the larger picture, the ability to visualize the future of the organization is expected. While the mission of the library is essential for defining the context of the organization at the outset, a "visualization" of the organization's future at this stage is essential.

The heart of strategic planning, the definition of future strategies that respond to the statement of the strategic issues or themes, is step six. What strategies will permit the library to meet opportunities and threats defined in the environmental analysis and to answer questions posed about future directions in the analysis of strategic issues? Where is the library going to direct its resources to achieve maximum results? The strategies are the key elements that will permit the library to define the future. A strategy that responds to the strategic issue defined in the previous step is, "Limit science journal acquisitions to a core list of 1,000 quality titles and supplement holdings through interlibrary borrowing." Below[27] makes a critical distinction. A strategy states where the library is going rather than how it is going to get there. Strategy differs from long-range planning, in that long-range planning extrapolates the present into the future without creating an idea of where we are going. Note that "strategies" should decisively influence the direction that the library takes. They should describe new access approaches, new services, or distinct new directions in collection development and management. They do not describe how the library gets to where it wants to go.

Step seven must deal with how the library gets to where it wants to go. This is the program level of the strategic planning process. Programs define the organizational activities required to carry out strategies. These are the activities that determine how the library will achieve its specified strategies. It is at this point that grassroots involvement of library staff will bear fruit. The individuals who will be charged with implementing strategic objectives must have a stake in the process; it is best achieved by soliciting program input and providing feedback prior to implementation. Nevertheless, management retains the decision-making responsibility and should negotiate conditions, timetable, and budget constraints relating to implementation. It is at the program level that budget and other resources must be considered. If management selects a strategic program at this point, we must presume that budget will be provided for implementation. Many strategic plans fail because they ignore the necessity for management to identify resources for programs or to make the hard choices required to implement necessary programs. Strategic planning, thus, retains the best of PPB if it links budget to the strategic program decisions that must be made to respond to environmental changes. Some comments about resource acquisition are included in a later section.

Finally, in the last step, implementation and provision for evaluation and shift of direction must be considered. Strategic programs will be implemented only by strong management resolve and staff commitment. Bryson[28] suggests that four issues must be considered during implementation.

- Human problems—How do new strategic programs affect staff and users? All participants must be committed and in agreement.

- Process problems—How is the "unconventional wisdom" of the strategic plan turned into "conventional wisdom" of the future?

- Structural problems—Be sure that all internal and external environments are linked.

- Institutional problems—How do we transform the library into a highly interactive organization with redefined purpose. Implementation of strategic programs provides the opportunity to establish new organizational purpose and integrity. Effective leadership can use strategic program implementation to eliminate organizational drift and to increase organizational competence.

Evaluation of new strategic programs must be ongoing and should be formally conducted at least annually. Since strategic planning is inherently flexible, management should take care to terminate new programs that do not achieve the desired results. Concomitantly, review provides the opportunity to identify new strategic issues and to implement new strategic programs at any time. This process of flexibility and renewal will make strategic planning most effective. We know that change can occur rapidly, and strategic planning responds to environmental change. Evaluation, consequently, provides the continuing opportunity for rapid change of direction.

RESOURCE ACQUISITION

Up to this point, strategic planning process steps have dealt loosely with the issue of budget. It has been suggested that since upper management controls the process, budget decisions can be made as necessary. A management team committed to strategic decision-making will, by definition, insure adequate budget for strategic programs. Nevertheless, how to obtain necessary resources for implementing strategic programs is an important issue for all participants. This is especially true because the acquisition of adequate resources may require that choices be made between existing and new programs. Consequently, this tactic and several others are discussed here.

Strategic planning is particularly well-suited to organizations where resources are declining or real growth is limited. Thus, to implement new programs, resources may only be available from existing library programs. In today's competitive economic environment, it would not be uncommon for astute management to conclude that the library has one hundred percent (or more) of all operating funds (adjusted for inflation) it will ever have. At the author's own institution, current strategic planning guidelines assume that ninety-five percent of all future funding is now available. It follows, therefore, that funding for strategic planning may have to come from a reallocation of existing resources. Serious strategic planning efforts, consequently, will eliminate, consolidate, or modify existing programs and reallocate resources to new strategic programs. This is a shocking issue for most library managers but it must be a realistic consideration. What program or function can be eliminated in order to implement an essential new program?

Another method for obtaining resources is to reallocate all inflationary incremental operating funds received to strategic programs. This strikes a fatal blow to incrementalism and provides the funding for new programs. In a large organization, this tactic can be a source of substantial revenues. However, repeated capture of incremental funds may have the effect of reducing effectiveness to the point where selective program elimination is a better alternative.

Next, management could assess all operating units a portion of existing resources and reallocate them to strategic programs. The scope of existing units can be modified or reduced by reassigning staff and operating funds to strategic programs. Management can return staff vacancies to a central pool instead of filling positions for the former unit. However, avoid "reverse incrementalism." Do not assess operating units and reallocate a percentage of resources on a continuing basis, to the point where effectiveness is compromised. Instead, use the option of eliminating or consolidating programs.

All libraries should consider the acquisition of new resources from non-traditional sources. In particular, publicly-funded libraries may have become complacent and may not have considered new sources of funding. Outside funding from governmental and private sources may be a new source of revenue. Appoint a development officer or grant writer to initiate fund-raising efforts. Become an entrepreneur or charge for library services. Increase the charges for existing library services.

Finally, libraries must compete for resources in the budget-making processes of the parent institution or governing unit. The library's strategic plan may be used as the vehicle for requesting funding for strategic initiatives. Proactive planning positions the library to appeal for new resources. The library may also be a strategic issue or program for the parent. If the parent organization is doing strategic planning, take advantage of "strategic program initiative" opportunities provided. If library strategic planning is done within the context of the parent institution's strategic planning, an astute library plan may position the library to compete for new funding.

All things considered, the creativity of a library's strategy in identifying funding sources for strategic initiatives may be as important as the programs themselves. In fact, resource acquisition is, more often than not, one of the library's strategies or programs.

CONCLUSION

To meet the challenges and uncertainties of the 1990's, library managers cannot continue the passive and reactive planning practices of the past. Rather, they must act proactively and creatively to develop an effective future for the organization. The principles, processes, and mindset of strategic planning provide the best means to insure a competitive, focused, and productive future. Some final comments about strategic planning should be helpful to library managers in beginning to think strategically and to plan formal strategic planning efforts for the library. Strategic planning,

- is an active, ongoing process and way of thinking that concentrates resources in areas that are most productive.
- anticipates the future and proposes those strategies that will permit the library to actively meet that future.
- provides a framework for making choices between what the library has always done and what the library must do to remain viable.
- is a tool of leadership that can build consensus within the library organization and promote understanding of and commitment to organizational purpose.
- must have outcomes that are directly related to current and expected resources.
- must be consistent with the mission and goals of the parent organization.
- leads to the expectation that programs may be modified or eliminated as a means of providing resources for new strategic programs.
- requires continuous updating and review.
- should be imbedded in library culture, thinking, and operations.

Finally, strategic planning is a productive endeavor for all types of libraries. It can be successfully done with a few basic guidelines and can be completed without formal training. However, its basic principles must be understood and the library manager must be prepared to make the difficult programmatic and budgetary decisions that are necessary. The 1990's will present considerable challenges from external forces. Libraries and librarians have a choice of creating the future or accepting consequences that the environment will determine.

REFERENCES

1. Russell L. Ackoff, *Creating the Corporate Future* (New York: John Wiley and Sons, 1981), p.51.
2. John M. Bryson, *Strategic Planning for Public and Nonprofit Organizations* (San Francisco: Jossey-Bass Publishers, 1988), p.117. Quotation attributed to Hubert H. Humphrey, *The Education of a Public Man: My Life and Politics* (New York: Doubleday, 1976).
3. Association of Research Libraries, *The Report of the ARL Serials Prices Project* (Washington, D.C.: Association of Research Libraries, 1989), p.10.
4. Kim A. McDonald, "Scientists Urged to Help Resolve Library 'Crisis' by Shunning High-Cost, Low-Quality Journals," *The Chronicle of Higher Education* (February 28, 1990), p.A6.
5. Association of Research Libraries, "Strategic Planning in ARL Libraries," *Spec Flyer 108* (Washington, D.C.: ARL, October, 1984), pp.i-ii.
6. Bryson, p.5.
7. George Keller, *Academic Strategy: The Management Revolution in Higher Education* (Baltimore: Johns Hopkins, 1983), p.143.
8. Barbara B. Moran, "Strategic Planning in Higher Education," *College and Research Libraries News* 46, no.6 (June 1985): p.290.
9. Bryson, p.7.
10. Moran, p.289.
11. Keller, p.101.
12. Keller, p.101.
13. Keller, p.102.
14. Charles L. Schultze, *The Politics and Economics of Public Spending* (Washington, D.C.: The Brookings Institution, 1968), pp.15-23.
15. Keller, p.106.
16. Bryson, pp.3-10.
17. K. J. Radford, *Strategic Planning: An Analytical Approach* (Reston, Virginia: Reston Publishing Co., Inc., 1980), pp.2-4.
18. National Commission on Excellence in Education, *A Nation at Risk* (Washington, D.C.: U.S. Government Printing Office, April, 1983), pp.8-10.
19. Keller, p.19.
20. Keller, pp.140-163.
21. Patrick J. Below, George L. Morrisey, and Betty L. Acomb, *The Executive Guide to Strategic Planning* (San Francisco: Jossey-Bass Publishers, 1987), pp.9-14.
22. Bryson, pp.46-70.
23. Bonita H. Melcher and Harold Kerzner, *Strategic Planning: Development*

and Implementation (Blue Ridge Summit, Pennsylvania: TAB Professional and Reference Books, 1988), pp.1-13.
   24. Bryson, p.73.
   25. Moran, p.289.
   26. Bryson, p.7.
   27. Below, p.56.
   28. Bryson, p.197.

Creativity and Innovation in an Organized Anarchy

Joan R. Giesecke

SUMMARY. Organizations can respond to change in their environments in a variety of planned and unplanned ways. In complex organizations, when the environment is unstable, managers need to examine their assumptions about how organizations function in order to develop effective strategies for introducing creativity and change. This essay reviews the assumptions behind theories of organizational decision making, explores how those assumptions affect how managers decide strategies for introducing change, and offers some ideas on how to introduce creativity into organizations that face ambiguous internal and external environments.

INTRODUCTION

Organizations can create their own futures and respond to changes in their environment in a variety of ways with planned and unplanned strategies. When the environment is relatively stable and predictable, organizations turn to planned change as a way for the organization to stay in tune with its environment. Planned changes emphasize rational, logical thought and decision making techniques. These processes focus on performance and management within the existing system. Planned change involves events that can be anticipated. It is a response to what is viewed as a closed system.

However, when organizations face an unstable environment and when their internal processes are also changing, a different approach to change may be needed. In this setting managers need to examine their assumptions about how organizations function in or-

---

Joan Giesecke is Associate Dean of Libraries at the University of Nebraska, Lincoln, NB.

der to develop effective strategies for introducing creativity and change into their organizations. This article will review the assumptions behind theories of organizational decision-making, will explore how those assumptions affect how managers decide strategies for introducing change, and will offer some ideas on how to introduce creativity into organizations that face ambiguous internal and external environments.

BACKGROUND

Classical theories of organizations emphasize rational thought and controlled, predictable actions. The rational model assumes that organizations have understandable, consistent goals which are used to guide organizational actions. In this model decision making consists of the following steps: the manager identifies a problem; identifies various alternatives for solving the problem; evaluates the alternatives based on organizational preferences or goals; and chooses an alternative that maximizes benefits for the organization. Recent empirical studies of organizational decision-making, however, portray a different, more confusing picture of organizations. Studies of managers' work in organizations found that the manager's job is inherently open-ended where planning is done haphazardly, work is fragmented, and interruptions are common.[1] Problems arrive in no particular order and are handled sequentially. Managers rarely consider rational objectives and planned strategies when deciding which problems to solve. Rather managers are likely to choose those problems which fit with the manager's own view of his/her role in the organization.

As theorists coped with the discrepancies between the classical model and the real world, the rational model as the ideal gave way to models of incrementalism and satisficing.[2] Incrementalists argue that most decisions consist of making small adjustments to the status quo. These incremental changes emerge from a bargaining process among decision makers where the best alternative is the one on which decision makers can agree, rather than being the alternative that necessarily maximizes benefits. Abstract goals and objectives are not debated. Instead decision makers focus on current programs and policies where adjustments can be made.

An alternative to the incremental model is found in the work of Herbert Simon and his approach known as satisficing. This model recognizes that decision makers have limited access to information and limited ability to process information. In this approach decision makers stop searching for alternatives as soon as an alternative is found which meets the manager's minimum acceptable goals. That is, the manager chooses the alternative that is sufficient or "good enough."

Still, these models could not account for all of the events that make up organizational decision-making. Recent studies of organizations have, in fact, questioned whether or not organizational goals can be known. These studies find that decision makers may not have well defined preferences. Alternative courses of action may not be well understood. The set of possible outcomes or solutions may not be well explicated.[3]

Furthermore, studies showed that participants appear and disappear in the organization, varying the amount of time they are willing to spend on any given issue. Problems seem to float in organizations and solutions may precede problem identification. Goals might be discovered after action had occurred. In other words, the simplified models of organizational choice did not explain much of what is observed in organizational settings.

These discrepancies, between observed behavior and theoretical models that are based on the assumption that goals guide actions, led James G. March, Michael Cohen and Johan Olsen to develop a different approach to use in describing organizational behavior in complex organizations.[4] They address the messiness of managerial decision making where identification of problems, discovery of alternatives, evaluation of solutions, and making of choices can occur together, vaguely, or not at all. They propose a model that characterizes organizations as organized anarchies. In this view they mean any organization that exhibits the following characteristics:

a. Problematic Goals. The organization appears to operate on a variety of inconsistent and ill-defined preferences.
b. Unclear Technology. The organizational members do not always understand organizational processes. The organization seems to run on a trial-and-error basis.

c. Fluid Participation. Participants in the organization vary among themselves in the amount of time and effort they devote to the organization.[5]

In such organizations as described above, ambiguity dominates and participants have varying ideas about what is happening or why it is happening. Individuals do not necessarily agree about organizational goals. They find themselves in a more complex and less stable world than is described in most standard theories of organizational behavior.

According to March and Olsen, in organizations that exhibit these characteristics, decision-making processes are messy and complex. They argue that problems, solutions, participants, and decision-making opportunities are separate entities that can exist independently within an organization. Problems, solutions, and participants can be viewed as streams that flow through an organization and may or may not come together in a decision-making opportunity. The decision-making opportunity is viewed as a garbage can where problems, solutions, and participants meet in no particular order. At that point the organization may choose to make a decision, to ignore all of the problems and solutions raised in the decision-making opportunity, or may choose to resolve other problems in the organization which were not part of the original decision-making opportunity or garbage can.

In this garbage can environment, there are no obvious rules for linking problems and solutions together to ensure that problems are resolved. It is difficult to examine organizational goals, objectives, rules and regulations, and predict which participants are likely to be present at any given meeting or decision-making opportunity or which problems or solutions may be raised. Decisions, then, will not be made through the traditional steps of identifying issues, examining alternatives, and proposing solutions. Rather, solutions may precede problems, and individual problems, solutions, or participants may appear in any number of decision-making opportunities.

The outcome of the decision-making process may not necessarily reflect the intentions of the participants. Outcomes are most likely to be the result of fortuitous timing rather than representing the explicit choice of the participants. The decision-making process in this model is a dynamic process, where problems, solution, and participants move throughout the organization and where events are not dominated by intention. Particularly in times of change, when an organization may face many problems at the same time, the intentions of participants are likely to be lost in the flow of problems, solutions, and people.

ACADEMIC LIBRARIES AS ORGANIZED ANARCHIES

Universities are prototypical organized anarchies, or organizations that fit the characteristics of March and Olsen's model. Institutional goals are vague, conflicting and rarely understood. Organizational processes are familiar, but not understood. The major participants in the organization, the faculty and students, wander in and out of the process, participating in organizational activities and decision-making opportunities only until they find something better to do with their time. The organizations do not function solely as hierarchies. Rather, the setting includes collegial elements of faculty governance, and individual faculty entrepreneurial behavior, blended with an administrative hierarchy.

Within the framework of the university, the academic library as a service unit also reflects the characteristics of an organized anarchy. Academic libraries have multiple goals which may be in conflict as the library serves its various patrons. Provision of service to undergraduates must compete with specialized resources needed to support faculty research. The desire to preserve a collection may be in conflict with the need to provide users with access to information. Each market the library serves may need different types of resources and different services. Furthermore professional standards may dominate organizational preferences rather than the goals of the organization guiding its activities.

Academic libraries also have unclear organizational technologies. That is, processes are not clearly understood by the library faculty and staff. There is little overall agreement in the field as to what services a library should provide or how these services relate to the outputs of the educational process.

Finally participation in decision making in academic libraries is a fluid process. As is true for the university as a whole, library faculty have various opportunities to participate in organizational decision making. Committee assignments, administrative responsibilities, as well as collegial bodies all offer faculty an opportunity to participate in the organization. However, because library faculty have competing demands on their time, they must decide to what extent they wish to participate in any given issue. Even once an initial decision is made on how much time to devote to an issue, their involvement may vary as other activities arise that capture their attention. In a complex organization where faculty are somewhat autonomous, it becomes difficult at best to predict with any certainty who is likely to stay involved in any particular decision-making opportunity.

COPING IN AN ORGANIZED ANARCHY

Given the complexity of the library organizations, in times of change, when elements of an organized anarchy are likely to be present, one is faced with the problem of how to effectively function within this ambiguous environment. Theorists have proposed three basic approaches for dealing with the anarchy predicted by March and Olsen's model:

1. Reform the process to make the organization conform more closely to classical, planned models.
2. Adapt to the process by developing strategies to work around the anarchy in the decision-making process.
3. Embrace the process by exploiting the advantages of the fluid environment that is the cornerstone of this model.[6]

Reform the Process

This first strategy is based on the belief that an organized anarchy is a muddleheaded, inefficient organization that is likely to fail. This strategy suggests that managers add rules and regulations to the organization to control the movement of problems, solutions, and participants and to limit the kinds of problems and solutions that can appear in the organization. Managers need to create an organizational environment that promotes rational decision-making and rational organizational structures. The development of an agreed to set of organizational values and beliefs can be used to hold the organization together so that decision-making processes do not deteriorate into the randomness of the garbage can model. Planned change strategies such as strategic planning exercises can be used to set a direction for the organization while increasing the rules and regulations that guide decision-making processes.

Adapt to the Process

This second strategy is a matter of adopting a managerial style that works with the confusion found in the decision-making process. Tactics such as setting deadlines, spending a lot of time on a problem, persisting with an issue, and managing unobtrusively can be effective in decreasing the random movement of problems, solutions, and participants and increasing the ability of a manager to influence the process. Participants can also introduce a large number of items or projects into the system in order to distract other participants so that they do not spend too much time on any given topic. In each case, these tactics center on an individual taking the initiative and adapting to the anarchial environment. Although these tactics are available to any one who wants to use them, generally people have more interesting things to do than to try to manage decision-making processes.[7]

Another version of adapting to an organized anarchy process provided by March and Cohen begins with the idea that managers need to think about organizations in complex ways that are not dependent upon pre-existing goals. They suggest that managers: "think of goals as hypotheses, subject to experimentation and doubt; treat intuition as real; consider inconsistencies between expressed values and behavior as transitory rather than as fact." Their argument is that by recognizing and accepting the ambiguity of an organized anarchy managers can begin to discover new ways to cope with the process.[8]

Embrace the Process

This third set of strategies has as its goal helping managers to increase flexibility in the organization by embracing the processes found in an organized anarchy. This third set is particularly interested in encouraging creativity and innovation and in developing open processes that maximize the ability of participants to generate new ideas. These strategies are appropriate when an organization is facing a changing environment and changing values.

First, to increase flexibility in the organization, managers may choose to consciously suspend rules and regulations and to suspend rational imperatives toward consistency in order to promote less rational, planned behavior in the exploration of new ideas. This tactic, where action precedes thought so that people act first and think later, is described by March and his colleagues as a way to increase play in the organization.

Play allows for experimentation in the organization. It relieves participants from the need to appear rational and allows for actions that may seem unintelligent or irrational in order to explore alternative ideas and concepts. Play allows participants to combine skills in novel sets to increase flexibility in the organization. For example, unstructured brainstorming sessions are one way to begin to allow for play in the organization. "What play does is unhook behavior from the demands of real goals. The person gets experience in combining pieces of behavior that would not be juxtaposed in a utilitarian world."[9] Of course, play is only a temporary suspension of rules. At some point the ideas and activities of participants will need to be incorporated into the formal organizational structure.

One caveat, however, in using tactics to promote playfulness in the organization is that the participants need to be willing to openly debate problems in the organization and to seek new approaches to examining issues. Without this willingness by participants the process of promoting play will be difficult at best. Participants must trust and believe that managers will seriously consider the ideas and suggestions that result from a non-rational process. Without that trust, participants are likely to view the process with some suspicion because the process is not an accepted part of more traditional approaches to organizational decision-making and behavior. To succeed in the organization, then, playfulness needs to be accepted and supported by all parties involved in the process and cannot easily be imposed by one group on another.[10]

A second set of strategies for encouraging creativity in organized anarchies involve taking advantage of unanticipated changes or crises in the environment as opportunities to review how the organization is responding to a changing environment. Here managers need to seek unstructured ways to gather information about the organization in order to learn what is really going on in the organization. They also need to look for ways to encourage the development of spontaneous processes that can cope with unanticipated changes in the environment. Such tactics as Management by Walking Around provide an avenue for managers to use in order to tap into the informal organizational structure.[11] Managers can use the informal organizational structure to gather information, to assess the environment, and to unobtrusively influence organizational processes.

Organizational designs can also be used to encourage the development of creative structures. Organic structures, in contrast to mechanistic, machine-age structures, allow for adaptation to unplanned change. Such designs as the use of task forces, small working groups, and temporary working groups, are all flexible structures that encourage adaptation to change. These groups can respond to a crisis, experiment with various projects, identify problems, propose solutions more quickly than traditional bureaucratic structures. The use of these types of groups can encourage entrepreneurship in the organization and can foster creativity while avoiding the need to impose rational, bureaucratic constraints on the process. The tactics can help participants move beyond cognitive limits of rationality to a different plane of hunches, dreams, and speculation to allow the organization to respond to the unknown in its environment.

Of course, with all of these options, coordination of actions is essential if the work of the groups is to benefit the organization. The groups will fail if management loses interest in them, does not take their work seriously, and ignores the work of the groups.

Taking a slightly different approach and looking at how people think about organizations, Karl Weick argues for processes that encourage participants to see organizations in novel ways. By learning to think of organizations as organized anarchies, garbage cans, and such, managers can move beyond the cognitive limits of the rational model to exploring different ways for bringing about change. If an organization is narrow in its vision or image of itself, it won't be able to make interesting changes in light of changes in its surroundings. "An organization that sees itself in novel images, images that are permeated with diverse skills and sensitivities, thereby is equipped to deal with altered surroundings when they appear."[12]

Weick goes on to suggest additional strategies managers can use to be effective in complex organizations. He suggests that managers not panic in the face of disorder because disorder may signal an effective process for coping with ambiguity. Too, Weick warns against overmanaging the organization. Not all things happen at once, so managers can intervene judiciously and still affect overall changes. Events take time and managers do not need to be involved in all phases of an operation for the project to proceed smoothly. Third, Weick argues that any action by the organization, even chaotic action, is better than inaction. This is because actions help clarify what an organization is doing. It provides tangible results for participants to analyze and understand. Next Weick notes that there are no simple solutions or answers. Problems evolve and rarely have a distinct beginning and ending. Interdependent systems result in open-ended issues. By addressing issues on a small scale, fine tuning the organization, and always looking for changes in the organization surroundings, managers are in a better position to adjust to changes and to keep the organization moving forward. Finally Weick argues that managers need to complicate their views of the organization to begin to recognize the ambiguous processes that hold the organization together. Most organizational models try to simplify the organization to a few key variables in an attempt to meaningfully explain organizational behavior. In contrast to this approach, Weick argues that, in complex organizations, this simplification process can lead to simple but inadequate answers to complex issues. By recognizing the messy, diverse confusion that typifies today's organizations, and realizing that organizations are processes rather than static entities, managers will be better able to develop and implement creative solutions to organizational problems. To bring creativity and innovation into the organization, managers need to "begin to take pleasure in the process rather than pleasure in the outcome."[13]

UTILITY OF THE MODELS

But in a practical sense, where does all this advice lead the manager of complex organizations? Should we abandon the prescriptions of the rational, traditional models for the nonrational, more fluid advice for managing organized anarchies? As our organizations become more complex and our environment continues to change in unanticipated ways, it becomes more evident that no one model will answer all of our concerns. Basically to succeed in complex organizations, we need to balance planned and unplanned strategies by using both rational and nonrational approaches to organizational decision making. We need a combination of reforming and adapting strategies along with strategies that embrace the messy processes that make up organized anarchies. To accomplish this, theorists such as Bo Hedberg, Paul Nystrom and William Starbuck advocate that we stop thinking of organizations as solid objects, and begin thinking of them as mobile tents.[14] The image of an organization as a tent emphasizes flexibility, creativity, immediacy, and initiative rather than authority, clarity, and decisiveness. Tents can easily move as the environment or foundation for the organization shifts. They can take advantage of those changes without destroying the fundamental structure of the organization. Realistically, few organizations are as flexible as tents. Nonetheless, in spite of the fact that most management theories emphasize rational thought and planned approaches to change, we do need to think in terms of adaptive, flexible structures that can stay balanced while coping with change. Balance is needed between a siege mentality where organizational actors seek to protect the structure, centralize authority, and solve short run crises with radical change that destroys the organization.

In our complex environment, balance is needed in six areas for the organization to succeed and survive. First, we need minimal consensus, or a balance between complete consensus and the dangers of group think, and open warfare or dissension. Between these extremes lies a middle ground of cooperation rather than complete cooptation. Second, we need minimal contentment, and a balance between complacency and discontentment. Organizational participants need to feel a part of the organization but not so comfortable that they are unmotivated to deal with change. Third, we need minimal affluence and a balance between excess resources that can lead to waste and such scarce resources that we can not function. Minimal faith in goals is also important. We need to balance our planning activities with the knowledge that we can not accurately predict the future. We want to plan for the future but not rely so on our plans that we lose sight of reality. Fifth, the organization needs minimal consistency and a balance between such slow evolution that nothing happens and a wide revolution that destroys the organization. Finally, we need minimal rationality and a balance between objectivity and ambiguity. A creative organization coping with change and creating its own future needs ambiguous authority structures, inconsistent statuses, overlapping responsibilities, competitive activities, volatile rules, and varying criteria for decision making. This less than efficient organization may not save resources, but the added flexibility and innovation will keep the organization afloat in a changing world.

CONCLUSION

In summary, a dynamic balance is needed between planning and overlapping, unplanned, nonrational processes to keep the organization current. Planned change strategies such as strategic planning help an organization decrease the anarchy in its processes and allow the organization to respond to identified changes in the environment. These processes encourage stability by considering known elements in the environment and incorporating them into the planning process. When they are done well they allow the organization to set its course in a changing environment. Badly done, however, they can lead to an organization drifting in the backwater of its environment, unable to respond creatively to change.

Unplanned change strategies that embrace the anarchy in the organization, allow the organization to move beyond the cognitive limits of rationality to a different level of hunches and dreams so that organizations can respond to the unknown in their environments and to create their own destinies. Successfully done these strategies can lead to innovative, creative organizations. Badly done they may lead to chaos.

NOTES

1. Henry Mintzberg, *The Nature of Managerial Work* (New York: Harper & Row, 1973).
2. See Charles Lindblom, "The Science of Muddling 'Through,'" *Public Administration Review* 19 (1957): 79-88 and Herbert Simm, *Administration Behavior* (New York: Free Press, 1976).
3. David Cooper and David Hayes, "Accounting in Organized Anarchies: Understanding and Designing Accounting Systems in Ambiguous Situations," *Accounting, Organization, and Society* 6 (1981): 176.
4. James G. March and Johan Olsen, *Ambiguity and Choice in Organization* (Bergen: Universitetstorlaget, 1979).
5. James G. March and Michael Cohen, *Leadership and Ambiguity* (Boston: Harvard Business School Press, 1986), p. 3.
6. James G. March and Roger Weissinger-Baylor, *Ambiguity and Command* (Massachusetts: Pitman Publishing, Inc., 1986), pp. 25-28.
7. James G. March and Michael Cohen, p. 215.
8. James G. March and Michael Cohen, p. 222.
9. Karl Weick, *Social Psychology of Organizing* (New York: Random House, 1979), p. 248.
10. Richad West, "Will Playfulness be Possible in University Management," *College Board Review* 112 (1979): 14-19.
11. Thomas J. Peters and Robert H. Waterman, Jr., *In Search of Excellence* (New York: Warner Books, (1982), p. 122.
12. Karl Weick, p. 249.
13. Karl Weick, p. 263.
14. Bo Hedberg, Paul Nystrom, and William Starbuck, "Camping on Seesaws: Prescriptions for a Self-Designing Organization," *Adminstrative Science Quarterly* 21 (1976): 41-65.

A New Leadership Paradigm: Empowering Library Staff and Improving Performance

Maureen Sullivan

SUMMARY. The critical steps to improved performance in organizations are the empowerment of staff and the meaningful involvement of staff at all levels of the organization. This calls for a new paradigm of leadership, the "acknowledge-create-empower" paradigm as developed by Evered and Selman. The author describes this model and its application to library organizations. The core values and leadership philosophy for empowering staff are explained. Sullivan suggests a number of strategies for library managers to consider as they increase the role of staff in library problem-solving and decision-making.

As the leaders of today's libraries consider how to create a future in which their libraries will offer the best possible services and programs to users with a limited or no increase in available resources, a critical area for their attention must be the staff. The largest segment of the allocated budget in most libraries is devoted to personnel resources. Much of the library manager's time is spent addressing a variety of personnel issues and problems. The time has come to transform the way in which administrators and supervisors work with and provide leadership to the staff in our libraries. This transformation requires a new philosophy of leadership, one that empowers staff and fosters creativity.

Evered and Selman offer a useful context for this new philosophy in their description of a new paradigm for the relationship between

---

Maureen Sullivan is Head, Library Personnel Services at Yale University, New Haven, CT.

the manager and staff. They call this the "acknowledge-create-empower" or ("a.c.e.") paradigm and suggest that its fundamental beliefs "have to do with rethinking our thoughts, aligned purpose, commitment to accomplishment, collaboration, involvement, mutual support, individual growth—in short, enabling the people in a group or team to generate results and to be empowered by the results they generate."[1]

Evered and Selman suggest this as an alternative to the traditional managerial philosophy that has been so prevalent in organizations, what they call the "control-order-prescriptive" ("c.o.p.") paradigm. Their description of the basic beliefs of this philosophy are the familiar ones of "being in charge, controlling others, implementing the owner's orders, prescribing behaviors and events, maintaining order, gaining and exercising command and control, and discarding the noncompliant."[2] The authors acknowledge that the transition from the "c.o.p." to the "a.c.e." paradigm is a difficult one, but they propose that the role of the manager as a coach is the appropriate strategy for this transition.

This coaching role for the manager in the context of the "a.c.e." paradigm requires a new definition of the term. This new meaning of coaching is one of a committed partnership. Evered and Selman describe it this way: ". . . a coach is someone who has an on-going, committed partnership with a player/performer and who empowers that person, or team, to exceed prior levels of play/performance."[3] The heart of coaching in this context is the relationship between the manager or leader and the staff member. The essential elements of this meaning of coaching are:

1. Partnership, mutuality, relationship
2. Commitment to producing a result and enacting a vision
3. Compassion, generosity, nonjudgmental acceptance, love
4. Speaking and listening for action
5. Responsiveness of the player to the coach's interpretation
6. Honoring the uniqueness of each player, relationship, and situation
7. Practice and preparation
8. Willingness to coach and be coached

9. Sensitivity to "team" as well as to individuals
10. Willingness to go beyond what's already been achieved.

Both this new meaning for the role of the manager as coach and the acknowledge-create-empower paradigm offer the leaders of today's libraries a means to create a future in which the organization's goals are met through the best performance of its staff. The staff are committed to excellence, assume responsibility for their performance, and develop to their full potential. To achieve this excellence, self-responsibility, and development, staff must have greater involvement in the problem-solving and decision-making activities of the library.

Coincidentally, the increasing use of automated systems for the accomplishment of work in libraries has led to the corresponding need for staff to solve a greater range and number of problems and for broader staff participation in decisions. Much of the work is now computer-mediated and requires more abstract thinking and more immediate problem-solving at the terminal. Library managers have less direct knowledge of the work they supervise and rely more on the staff doing this work to solve problems as they occur and to make decisions on-the-spot. There is not time to refer all problems arising from work activities to the manager for decisions, nor is the manager now able to make these decisions. Frequently it is the staff who are doing the work who have the necessary information and more relevant experience for solving many of today's work problems. As the manager's role shifts from one of direction and control to one of guidance and coordination, the role of staff shifts from that of a subordinate to a partner or participant in the accomplishment of work and the achievement of organizational goals. This new role for staff requires greater, more effective participation.

SUGGESTED PRINCIPLES FOR MEANINGFUL STAFF INVOLVEMENT

Lawler describes several assumptions about people in organizations that are fundamental to the effective and meaningful participation of staff:[4]

Human Relations

People should be treated fairly and with respect.

People want to participate.

When people participate, they accept change.

When people participate, they are more satisfied and committed to the organization.

Human Resources

People are a valuable resource because they have ideas and knowledge.

When people have input in decisions, better solutions are developed.

Organizations should make a long-term commitment to the development of people because it makes them more valuable to the organization.

High Involvement

People can be trusted to make important decisions about their work activities.

People can develop the knowledge to make important decisions about the management of their work activities.

When people make decisions about the management of their work, the result is greater organizational effectiveness.

These are a general set of assumptions that would effectively support a model for greater staff involvement in the library. The individual library and its staff should articulate its own set of assumptions. This process of clearly articulating the guiding principles or organizational philosophy and values has proven to be a critical step for successful organizations. Of course, it's also important that members of the organization, especially its appointed leaders, act in accordance with the espoused principles.

LEADERSHIP BEHAVIORS FOR THE EMPOWERMENT OF STAFF

The "acknowledge-create-empower" paradigm with its new meaning for the coaching role and the principles for "high-involvement management" suggests a set of critical behaviors for the effective leader of staff in this new environment. As Lawler says, "the key positions need to be staffed by leaders. Traditional managerial behaviors are not needed. . . . Leadership, however, is needed to provide a sense of purpose and direction as well as to shape the organization's culture and decision processes."[5]

First and foremost, leaders believe that staff are capable members of the organization who are committed to its success and who will work towards that success. Leaders act on this belief as they carry out their everyday responsibilities and in their on-going interactions with staff. Leaders create many opportunities for staff to participate in decisions and also to exercise leadership. They encourage a shared leadership in which staff assume a mutual responsibility for high performance.

Leaders articulate a vision of the organization that provides a sense of direction and purpose. This vision is important to staff at all levels of the organization. The library director provides the vision for the library as a whole, while the department head defines a vision for the department that is consistent with the overall vision. The vision guides both the leader and the staff in setting goals and objectives for performance. It also describes a preferred future for the library or department and suggests the role of staff in getting there.

The engagement of staff in this shared leadership is recognized as an evolutionary process and one that requires careful attention to the developmental level of staff. Because the various members of the staff are seen as the different individuals that they are, it is understood that they are at varying levels of development. The effective leader helps each person to perform at their current level of development while continuing to develop their skills and abilities.

As staff develop, leaders gradually share more responsibility. As new skills are learned, greater independence of action is encouraged and more responsibility is delegated. The Hersey/Blanchard model of Situational Leadership[6] suggests a continuum of four different, but progressive, leadership styles that match a corresponding continuum of developmental levels for staff. In the early stages of the leader/staff relationship, the appropriate style for the leader is a highly directive one to match the needs of the new, inexperienced staff member who has limited understanding of organizational goals and who requires considerable structure and direction from the leader. As the staff member develops an understanding and commitment to the overall goals represented in the work, gains experience, assumes greater responsibility, and becomes a competent performer, the leader gradually moves through the continuum of styles to the fourth stage, the leader as developer.

A new approach to problem-solving is adopted. Problems are seen as opportunities for the staff and the leaders alike to learn and to develop their skills and abilities. Mistakes are recognized as a natural consequence of work in an organization. The increased complexity in the work and the systems designed for the accomplishment of this work have created new problems, many of which are quite complex. The leader recognizes that problem-solving is both a technical process and one that furthers the development of those who participate. When things go wrong or failures occur, the leader takes time to study why. This is done for the purpose of learning, not assigning blame. This "post-mortem" is an early stage in the problem-solving process. The leader assures that staff move forward to solve the problem and do not become distracted at this early stage.

The leader focuses on empowering others by encouraging self-responsibility and shared responsibility in the enterprise. Work assignments and special projects are delegated whenever possible. Performance expectations are clearly stated and set mutually by the leader and staff. Standards for competent levels of performance are known and understood by all staff. Staff are strongly encouraged to assess their own performance on an ongoing basis, to take corrective action as necessary, and to ask for help when needed. Staff are encouraged to make decisions when they can. They are trained to know when they can't. This empowerment represents a shift away from a dependent relationship to one of interdependence.

Every decision to hire, promote, offer a special assignment, or delegate work is based on a careful assessment of the person's skills and abilities for performing the work. As the work changes, the leader monitors the person's ability to perform new tasks and grow with the job. The leader intervenes as appropriate and, if necessary, changes the assignment or removes the person from that job. Performance problems are addressed as soon as they occur. The leader focuses on the performance problem, encourages staff to solve the problem, and provides support and guidance as needed. Bradford and Cohen[7] describe their method of "supportive confrontation" as one in which a manager deals directly with a performance problem by giving specific, timely feedback to the employee in a caring, supportive way.

The considerable, complex change that characterizes organizational life today creates a high degree of ambiguity. Leaders must manage this ambiguity. Belasco[8] suggests that "MTBS < MTMD," i.e., the mean time between surprises is less than the mean time for making decisions. That is, problems arise so frequently, there isn't enough time to devote to a thorough study of each. This is an apt description for organizational life in libraries. In this uncertain environment, leaders must be able to determine when they know enough to proceed to make a decision, even though they may not have all the information they would like.

The effective leader is a skilled communicator who routinely uses a variety of methods for communication in both the formal and the informal networks of the library. The informal network, or the "grapevine," is seen as an important complement to whatever formal mechanisms or structures exist. The leader regularly interacts with staff throughout the library, sharing information as well as receiving it. Important information is communicated more than once and by different methods. Major changes are announced well before they are implemented and staff reactions and ideas are encouraged.

The new leadership paradigm calls for different organizational structures, ones that are flexible and open to change. Leaders must question whether the current structures are effective. Do they facilitate or hinder effective performance, timely decisions, a healthy work environment in which staff are highly motivated and committed, and achievement of the overall vision and goals of the library?

The encouragement of decision-making at the lowest levels possible suggests fewer management levels. Increased participation in problem-solving and decision-making indicates a greater use of groups or teams.

STRATEGIES FOR DEVELOPING HIGH PERFORMANCE AND EMPOWERING STAFF

Develop Teams

Bradford and Cohen[9] call for the development of "mature, shared-responsibility teams" that would provide for coordination of the group's work among the members of the team, achieve high-quality solutions to complex problems, and share in the responsibility for achieving the highest quality of performance. Hackman[10] has defined a model of work groups that suggests the self-managing team as an effective structure for increasing employee commitment to quality performance. Peters[11] advocates the self-managing team as "the basic organizational building block."

Lowell and Sullivan[12] describe their experience with the introduction of self-managing teams in a library. The self-managing team is, in fact, "the basic building block" for the new organizational structure in Technical Services at the Yale University Library. Teams of librarians and support staff are organized around major subject and language areas for the full processing of materials added to the collection.

Train and Develop Staff for Now and the Future

The skills and abilities required for work in today's library environment is different from those required even five years ago. This pattern of change will continue. Most of the staff now working in our libraries will be working for us five or more years from now. An investment must be made in this important resource by training and retraining staff. Retraining has become as important to a quality staff development program as initial training.

Libraries are approaching a point at which retraining will be a consistant need. As the librarians' roles and responsibilities evolve to meet the new demands of a changing user population, so too will the roles and responsibilities of the support staff. Clerical work is being replaced by new and different kinds of technical work brought about by the various automated systems. More support staff are asked to perform higher level tasks, some at a professional level different from that performed by the librarian. All of this calls for a much greater investment in training and well-supported in-house programs to assure quality training is provided as it is needed.

Training programs will have to address both current and emerging needs. The implementation of integrated systems has demonstrated the importance of attending to emerging needs. The best training plans have not been able to identify all the training needs at the start. New needs have surfaced as training has occurred.

The increased involvement of staff in problem-solving and decision-making requires training in problem-solving methods, working in groups, managing conflict, critical thinking, and influencing skills. The new leadership paradigm calls for special training for those appointed to management positions, especially in the skills and abilities for empowering and developing staff.

Peters lists ten elements of successful training programs of the future:[13]

1. Extensive entry-level training that focuses on exactly the skills in which you wish to be distinctive.
2. All employees are treated as potential career employees.
3. Regular retraining is required.
4. Both time and money are generously expended.
5. On-the-job training counts too.
6. There are no limits to the skills that can profitably be taught to everyone.
7. Training is used to herald a commitment to a new strategic thrust.
8. Training is emphasized at a time of crisis.
9. All training is line-driven (line staff determine content and participate in the training).
10. Training is used to teach the organization's vision and values.

Libraries are obviously limited in their ability to incorporate fully all of these elements. Number 4 is difficult because so few dollars are allocated for training. Number 6 is somewhat constrained by the classification structures of the larger organization. Number 9 may be difficult because of the demands of the day-to-day operation or by line supervisors who have limited interest in training or lack the ability to train. These ten elements, however, represent a framework for designing the library's training program.

Plan and Assess Performance

Clearly written and meaningful performance goals, objectives, and standards are key to successful individual performance and a highly motivated staff. A performance planning process that focuses on planning for future improvement and development is the most important strategy for improved performance. Full staff involvement in setting goals and objectives can be an important way to build the working relationship with staff and to encourage self-responsibility for work performance. Open, honest communication on the part of both staff and supervisors is critical for accurate assessment of performance and for developing a foundation of trust.

Lead by Example

Bear in mind that staff have many opportunities to observe managers in action. They are often the first to notice a gap between what a manager says and what a manager does. Instilling new values, such as those suggested for "high-involvement" management, takes time and a consistent pattern of behavior by managers. Leadership or managerial philosophy, and the corresponding values, are communicated to members of the organization through the behavior of its leaders.

Analyze Current Patterns of Work and Redesign Jobs

Step back and review how the work of the library or individual department is organized. Review current work assignments. Talk to staff about what they enjoy doing, what they don't enjoy, what they think doesn't need to be done anymore, and what ideas they may have for improving the workflow. Consider new ways to organize the work and possible new assignments for staff that would introduce more variety and challenge into their work.

Define Career Paths

Work with other managers and colleagues to identify possible opportunities for promotion as well as transition jobs that would help staff to gain the skills and experience necessary for advancement. Provide individual career counseling that considers opportunities within the library or department as well as others outside the library.

Manage Ambiguity

Clarify as much as possible. Be patient with staff when they are slow to understand or accept a major change. Create as much lead time as possible for the implementation. This will help staff to adjust. It may also allow better information to become available. Initiate major changes in incremental stages. Use pilot projects or tests. Tell staff what is known and what isn't known in a given situation. Encourage them to voice their concerns and to express their feelings. Remind staff that learning is a natural part of organizational life and that change brings new discoveries.

Hire the Best Possible Staff

Hire new staff who can perform the work required of the current vacancy and who have the potential to contribute to the broader organization. Look for individuals who will function effectively in a changing environment and who will grow and develop. Involve staff in the interview and selection process. This early involvement is likely to lead to a more successful introduction of the new staff person to the work setting. It also creates an opportunity for applicants to learn more about the specific work activities of the position. Give a complete description of the work and its requirements to applicants. Take time to explain the broader goals and values of the library. View each job applicant as a potential new member of the library system, not just someone who might fill the current vacancy.

Review Personnel Policies and Systems

The library's personnel program should be designed to facilitate achievement of its overall goals and the effective performance of every staff member. Examine current policies and procedures in terms of whether they help or hinder the library and its staff. Regularly review these policies and programs such as recruitment, performance assessment and staff development to determine how they might be improved. Actively involve staff in these reviews.

Reward Success, Acknowledge Achievement, and Praise Effort

Feedback on successful performance is every bit as important as feedback on problems. Take time to recognize staff achievements, personally and publicly. Involve staff in the design of a formal recognition program for the library that would include different ways of acknowledging successful performance. Remember the importance of psychological rewards as well as monetary ones. Tie actual levels of performance to salary increases in a pay-for-performance system. Provide support and praise to staff who make a concerted effort to learn new skills and to perform at higher levels. Make sure that the standards for performance are explicit and known to all staff.

Attend to Your Own Development

As staff learn, adapt, and develop in the new organization, so should leaders. Know yourself and your characteristic leadership behaviors. Assess your primary leadership style by completing one of the several inventories available for this purpose. Attend training seminars and workshops that are designed to develop leadership skills and promote better self-awareness. Keep abreast of developments and trends in the library, its parent organization, the community and beyond. Learn to scan the external environment for information that will guide internal decisions. Plan your career by thinking of new possibilities rather than identifying a set path.

Change is complex, but it offers opportunity. It is also an evolutionary process that needs to be managed. Clearly, the responsibility for managing the considerable change underway in libraries rests with the formal leadership of those libraries. The staff, especially the array of informal leaders throughout the organization, are a vital resource. The effective leader will release, rather than control, the energy from this important resource. Meaningful participation, empowerment, and the on-going development of staff at all levels are the critical tasks of leadership today.

NOTES

1. Roger D. Evered and James C. Selman, "Coaching and the Art of Management," *Organizational Dynamics*, 18 (Autumn 1989): 18.
2. Ibid.
3. Ibid., 21.
4. Edward E. Lawler, *High-Involvement Management* (San Francisco: Jossey-Bass Publishers, 1986), 192-193.
5. Ibid., 209-210.
6. Paul Hersey and Kenneth K. Blanchard, *Management of Organizational Behavior: Utilizing Human Resources*, 4th ed. (Englewood, N.J.: Prentice Hall, Inc., 1982).
7. David L. Bradford and Allan R. Cohen, *Managing for Excellence: The Guide to Developing High Performance in Contemporary Organizations* (New York: John Wiley & Sons, 1984), 146.
8. James R. Belasco, presentation at the "How to Get the Very Best . . ." program sponsored by the Public Library Association, March 21, 1990, Chicago, IL. Belasco is the author of *Teaching the Elephant to Dance: Empowering Change in Your Organization* (New York: Crown Publishers, 1990).
9. Bradford and Cohen, op. cit., 173.
10. J. Richard Hackman, "The Psychology of Self-Management in Organizations," in *Psychology and Work: Productivity Change and Employment*, ed. M.S. Pollack and R.O. Perloff (Washington D.C.: American Psychological Association, 1986), 85-136.
11. Tom Peters, *Thriving on Chaos: Handbook for a Management Revolution* (New York: Harper & Row, 1988), 357.
12. Gerald R. Lowell and Maureen Sullivan, "Self-Management in Technical Services: The Yale Experience," *Library Administration & Management* (Winter 1989): 20-23.
13. Peters, op. cit., 391-394.

The Price of Partnership

Helen L. Gater

SUMMARY. The library's partnership in the academic enterprise is a worthy goal, but the pursuit of partnership extracts a price. This article describes the individual and organizational costs, as well as the dividends, identified by the Arizona State University West Campus Library as it has taken advantage of unique opportunities to play a partnership role.

> "He does possession keep,
> And is too wise to hazard partnership."
>
> —John Dryden

Since the beginning of the library instruction movement, librarians have sought a partnership role in the educational enterprise, but faculty and academic institutions are still reluctant to hazard partnership. Faculty maintain sole ownership of academic program and course development, instruction, assessment of student progress, academic standards, definition of academic mission, research agendas and governance. Student Affairs has ownership of recruitment, career counseling, and the array of training offered in academic survival skills. External Relations controls the community relations efforts. The need to recognize the library's role in contributing to the educational mission of the university has been the subject of numerous publications, some of the most recent and compelling of which are listed in the bibliography.

Helen L. Gater is Director of the Library of the West Campus of Arizona State University, Phoenix, AZ.

The author wishes to acknowledge the librarians of the West Campus of Arizona State University. This article describes their efforts and achievements and incorporates their comments about their pursuit of partnership.

© 1991 by The Haworth Press, Inc. All rights reserved.

When Arizona State University created its West Campus branch in 1984, the library was the first program to be established, serving students of what was, initially, nothing more than a concentration of off-campus classes offered by the parent institution. Rudimentary forms of other support services were quickly implemented, and academic administrators were then hired. The first resident faculty arrived three years after the library opened, and their number has doubled each year with new recruits from across the country. While meeting their instructional responsibilities and maintaining their research, this nucleus of faculty has simultaneously faced an extraordinary level of service obligations consisting of curriculum planning and development, faculty recruitment, development of governance processes, creation of the organizational infrastructure, planning of facilities, and community relations. This unstructured, rapidly changing and intensely demanding environment provided the opportunity for librarians to participate in academic affairs to an unusual degree because our numbers were needed to share the load. It was an opportunity which I welcomed. Having observed the variety of approaches that librarians have tried over the years to achieve academic recognition and acceptance, I had developed the conviction that we could best achieve confirmation as academic colleagues through application of our unique professional knowledge and skills outside the library as well as within. As the motivation and the opportunity converged, establishing a partnership with faculty became a primary objective of the ASU West Campus Library. This article describes our pursuit of partnership and offers some observations for those who may want to make a similar investment.

LEARNING THE BUSINESS

Pursuing partnership is both a political and an educational process. If we wish to gain interest in the enterprises that are owned and controlled by faculty, we must provide convincing evidence of the benefits of our participation. Before we can convince, or educate, we must first gain access. That process is political, the most important strategy of which is to understand the values, culture and traditions of the academy from the perspective of the faculty. This approach compares to the military strategist's goal of knowing the enemy or the salesperson's knowledge of clients and the competition.

Faculty, being very focused within their disciplines, tend to be insular and to view the world from their position in it; that view historically does not include librarians in a partnership role. In fact, the only role many faculty perceive librarians to have is a negative one: we make and enforce rules that restrict their use of library materials; we cancel their journals, or refuse to buy them in the first place, or impose the inconvenience of microforms.

To change the world view of faculty requires that we first expand our own. Librarians also tend to be insular: to look at services, collections, policies and procedures from the internal perspective of the library. We frequently see other functions of the university only from the standpoint of how the library is affected. Changing from a library-focused perspective to a more global one is not an easy adjustment, but the less we focus on the library itself, the easier it is to see and describe its role in the larger universe of teaching, research, recruitment, retention, and learning.

Each librarian, not just those with administrative responsibilities, needs to develop that external perspective to have a basis for effective participation. A good way to acquire an overview of academic structure, politics and issues of current interest nationally is to add books and journals on higher education to our list of professional reading materials. Knowing the agendas of our own institutions requires monitoring the local news media, reading reports and minutes produced within the institution, and having direct representation or secondary contacts on standing and ad hoc committees.

To know our own faculty, nothing can take the place of spending informal time developing personal relationships. We find that faculty, like librarians, often feel powerless, and that they question whether their contributions are fully appreciated. The stress that faculty experience from juggling teaching, research, advising, and committee work is similar to ours as we struggle to balance our commitments to reference, collection development, library instruction, service, and professional contributions. For librarians, this personalized understanding and empathy is a powerful antidote for any feelings of jealousy, envy or inferiority—attitudes that frequently color our perception of faculty and of our own status. As faculty simultaneously learn to appreciate our similarities, they can more readily accept librarians as true academic colleagues.

The personal relationships between librarians and faculty generate mutual respect and an appreciation of the strengths that are unique to each of our professions. Faculty are critical, independent thinkers and rank individualists. Conversely, the traditions of librarians emphasize group process, consistency, and the welfare of the whole over that of the individual. It is precisely those traits of faculty that permit them to excel as teachers and researchers, while the traditional characteristics of libraries foster valuable talents for working together, considering multiple points of view, spanning boundaries, reaching consensus, and using the organizational structure productively. By recognizing even our differences as organizational assets we gain an appreciation for what we can achieve as colleagues. Conflicts are more easily avoided or resolved, and by collaborating, we compensate for each other's weaknesses.

INVESTMENTS

The primary investment that is required for a partnership with faculty is acceptance of full responsibility for our own role — and for changing it. All too often, librarians look to the faculty leaders (committee chairs, senate presidents, etc.) and administration to provide equal access to participative roles, but in the academic milieu, power is dispersed among the faculty. The position we seek is not one which can be bestowed by edict.

While the focus needs to be outside the library, the process begins within. Clearly, the library's investment in partnership is far beyond the resources of a few individuals. To succeed, it must be an explicit and shared priority of the entire library organization. Library administrators can create opportunities, but they cannot win partnership by themselves. They can block the process, however. Individual librarians can achieve successes, but what one individual can achieve is limited to her/his span of influence. For example, a librarian who wins respect and credibility for quality of research instruction might be invited by a department to participate in the development or refinement of research methods courses, but unless this success is used as a prototype by others, the benefits are limited. Partnership in the academic enterprise requires the concerted and coordinated efforts of each library administrator and each librarian along with the collaboration of support staff.

Some of the costs of pursuing partnership relate to this need for organizational commitment. Organizations can effectively handle only a small number of true priorities, so the choice of partnership as a priority will mean limiting the efforts and resources spent in other directions. ASU West had an advantage by starting with new staff, who were selected in part because they shared the enthusiasm for developing an enhanced role for the library and themselves. Lacking an organizational history, priorities and resource allocations could be freshly established rather than shifted from old to new.

To change priorities and roles within an existing organization inevitably generates internal conflicts, but the process of choosing and implementing a mission that encompasses the entire organization is also an opportunity for team building. At ASU West, the professional staff meets twice monthly as the "Program Improvement Council." In this forum, we try to erase the hierarchical distinctions and communicate as colleagues. Discussions of what we are attempting to accomplish, and why, establish a sense of shared values as well as provide direction. Developing and sharing the institutional awareness and personal skills needed to advance the pursuit of partnership, that is, devising strategies, analyzing obstacles, celebrating victories, exchanging information and ideas, are communication processes that build a sense of shared mission and mutual respect.

Empowerment of librarians is a prerequisite to their partnership with faculty, but the hierarchical tradition of libraries dies a slow, hard death. Although on a much smaller scale, it can be compared to the democratic changes taking place in those Eastern European countries which lack a democratic tradition.

When the primary role of libraries was to build and manage a collection, the hierarchical structure served well to ensure consistency of policies, efficiency of technical processes, and quality of services which at that time were strictly in-house. In today's information age, little is centralized. The "collection" is the world wide information base, and services are dispersed. The emphasis is on the user's choices and evaluation of information, on providing access and guidance rather than merely providing material. This change has provided the opening for a more dynamic partnership between librarians and faculty, but taking advantage of the opening requires shifting the locus of power from library administrators to librarians as facilitators.

Democratizing the library is an evolving process of education with increasing delegation of accountability and control, and it carries a certain degree of risk and discomfort for everyone. A responsibility of the director is to be certain that everyone understands institutional politics, current issues, and administrative strategy; to risk the exposure created by such openness requires a sizeable measure of trust in one's colleagues.

The shift of power is perhaps most difficult for mid-level administrators. The director retains a clear leadership role. Mid-level administrators, who have traditionally been squeezed between the limitations and directives imposed from above and the expectations and demands from below, now have an even more ambiguous role and less power to share. The democratic environment requires mid-level administrators to continue to provide leadership while encouraging individual initiative and creativity, to be good coaches without calling all the shots, to be master coordinators and communicators, and to find as much reward in the empowerment of others as in their own achievements.

For non-administrative librarians, the shift is not easy either, but the advantages are the ability to effect change and to have an individual and vital stake in how the library performs its role. The price that librarians pay is risking greater accountability and exposure, learning to deal with positive confrontation and conflict as a normal by-product of peer decision making, and living with ambiguous boundaries as a new structure is defined.

At all levels, the transition of accountability and control is difficult to manage. As power, or control, is dispersed, accountability still rests squarely on the library administrators. In curricular matters, the institution recognizes the responsibility of the faculty. The responsibilty of librarians for library programs is not yet as well established.

Like administrators who have difficulty learning to delegate authority, many non-administrative librarians have difficulty learning to accept accountability. Participation in organizational decision making is much more pleasant than justifying to faculty the decisions that are unpopular. Relative autonomy in structuring the individual approach to the job and managing the work schedule must not be interpreted as freedom from accountability to peers, administration, and the institution as a whole.

A good organizational planning process and standards by which individual and organizational performance can be measured take on greater importance as methods of maintaining accountability. The organizational priorities become the framework within which individuals have considerable freedom to establish their own priorities. Similarly, having common standards provides a framework for individual approaches to achieving an objective.

STRATEGIES

Knowledge and understanding of the academic community needs to be applied formally and deliberately to have maximum effect on how our role is defined. The strategies used by ASU West librarians are the familiar ones: serving on committees, providing research instruction, publicizing services, serving as liaison to specific disciplines. The differences are in how those strategies are used: the amount of time and effort invested externally, the initial preparation, the language of communications, the opportunistic approach, and the expectations of results. In addition, an earnest effort is made to use the information and understanding that we acquire externally to counter stereotypes as well as to improve programs and delivery of services.

In most libraries, serving with faculty on committees is a standard form of participation that librarians choose because of their own interests and agendas; the quality of their participation is considered the business of the individual librarian and the committee. In a library that actively pursues partnership, participation is not a choice. Librarians are expected to find such opportunities, and the quality of their participation is of great interest to their library colleagues, because positive contributions enhance the cause of all, while passive membership or inept representation wastes an opportunity, at best. While librarians are subjected to peer pressure to meet these expectations, they also have the experience, knowledge, and advice of their colleagues to rely on; as a result, librarians devote considerable time to mentoring each other.

At ASU West, librarians who have served on faculty search committees have a greater awareness of standards for faculty, how they are judged, and how faculty build their careers. Experiencing those values through the search process helps to explain the faculty's allegiance to their individual disciplines, which is a key to understanding many of their behaviors. The fact that a librarian was involved in the selection process also has an impression on candidates — an impression that is underscored when newly hired faculty, before their arrival, receive a letter of welcome from their liaison librarian which briefly describes library services and offers to expedite any materials that will be needed for instruction in the fall.

Serving on a college resource committee has enabled one librarian to present library services as resources available to the faculty of the college. Although these same services had been widely advertised, presenting them in a new context imbued them with greater relevance and value.

The library's representative on the campus-wide faculty and academic professional personnel committee has the opportunity to draw parallels between those groups as policies and procedures are developed. By maintaining the maximum possible similarity with faculty, librarians avoid being considered enigmas in academic affairs and our governance procedures gain credibility because they share a common philosophy and language. The cost of conforming with faculty procedures is sometimes the sacrifice of library traditions. For example, our library search committees now are comprised strictly of peers with attention to the balance between tenured and untenured librarians. This does not mean that administrators are excluded from the process, but it does symbolize greater peer responsibility.

While librarians go about their traditional duties, they are expected to be alert for opportunities to participate in the academic enterprise, to be aware of what opportunities the library is prepared to act on, and to exercise initiative and ingenuity in gaining entry. Assisting a faculty member with research related to curriculum planning provided one librarian with the opportunity to volunteer to participate in the design of a new class which will include segments taught by librarians. While participating in a college curriculum committee, another librarian seized the opportunity to integrate the mastery of defined library skills into the teacher education curriculum.

Assertive marketing of the library is a new responsibility for most librarians and requires development of special skills, including learning to deal with rejection. Having the responsibility for the delivery of the services that they are marketing, librarians experience concerns about keeping up with the expectations that are being created and maintaining the level of quality that they, as well as their clientele, expect. In an environment where resources always lag behind demand, it requires an act of faith to encourage more demand. The librarian's credibility is directly at risk.

At ASU West, librarians have been assigned as liaisons to faculty of specific disciplines. An unusual element of this relationship, and a prime opportunity for the library, is the degree of reliance of faculty on library services. The collection, although growing rapidly, is very incomplete, especially for faculty research. Many of the sources faculty require must be obtained from the parent campus or elsewhere. The extensive use of electronic access tools requires new research strategies. Adding to these potential impediments to research is the lack of graduate assistants, a result of a high percentage of older adult part-time students. The library service programs must compensate for the lack of comprehensive collections and built-in research assistants, and the liaison librarian is the channel through which faculty obtain services. Liaison librarians also serve as advocates both for the faculty and the library. Complaints from the faculty offer librarians the opportunity to negotiate and take credit for desired changes and the responsibility to provide a positive explanation when requests cannot be accommodated. These opportunities require that librarians know, or find out about, policies and procedures outside their immediate functional areas, participate in problem solving across the organization, and take responsibility for communicating other library programs.

Serving as very visible external representatives of the library puts librarians "on the line" publicly. The rewards are greater power and recognition, but the cost is exposure, and it is shared by librarians and library administration alike. Traditionally, the administration has spoken for the organization; with more spokespersons, communication concerning the library is more pervasive, but it cannot be controlled. Good communication within the organization is a necessary base for accurate, consistent, and positive communication externally.

Throughout this article, little has been mentioned about the university's students; the price of partnership would, indeed, be too dear if students were neglected. Maintaining quality information services within the library while pursuing partnership externally requires a careful assessment of levels of complexity of services provided to different client groups and a dynamic and interactive partnership with paraprofessional information providers. The client groups are traditional—faculty, students and community users— and they have the traditional information needs ranging from simple information gathering to complex research. To apportion precious professional time, librarians concentrate on services to faculty and to all categories of clientele engaged in complex research. Paraprofessionals assist all categories of clientele who are gathering information for less complex purposes. Librarians provide course-integrated instruction and comprehensive research seminars. Paraprofessionals provide the ongoing instruction to individual information seekers and conduct seminars that focus on selected electronic tools.

Distinguishing these levels is not simple, as any reference librarian knows, and maintaining quality information service is a concern. So, although librarians are released from a substantial amount of routine and repetitive functions, they must devote time to training and mentoring of paraprofessionals. Training consists of reference interviewing, research strategy, knowledge of sources, use of specific tools, and the all-important referral. It also includes sensitizing paraprofessionals to their unique vantage point and the importance of their feedback to the quality of service and collections.

For librarians, there are personal and professional costs of delegating so much of what has traditionally been their responsibility. There are concerns about quality of service, losing some of their own reference skills, and not having the first-hand, front-line perspective of user needs.

One's security is also threatened when the familiar pattern and structure of work changes substantially. Librarians are no longer subject to the domination of the desk schedule, although they do maintain office hours. They are more in control of their own schedules and priorities, but the choices are difficult. Without a desk schedule, they have no scheduled "off desk" time, so they must continuously juggle time for collection development, course preparation, service obligations, a variety of formal and informal liaison activities, and requests for research assistance.

Although the academic division is the primary focus of the library's attention, student affairs and external relations also receive their share. As an upper level institution, ASU West recruits students from the neighboring community colleges as well as from the general adult community. In support of student recruitment and the institution's efforts to improve communication with community colleges, the library has initiated collaboration with the community college librarians and special privileges for their students. On our own campus, the library has served as a formal advocate for a variety of "quality of campus life" amenities needed by students.

In a large suburban area such as ours, removed by distance and traffic from the city's cultural amenities, a new academic institution and its library attract enormous interest from the community. The library has responded to community demand with a high degree of sensitivity to the community relations factor. Librarians are on call to host a rather continuous stream of visitors: young children, retirees, business and civic groups, legislators, potential donors, etc. As representatives of the institution, librarians must be prepared to speak to institutional issues and to avoid political quicksand, as well as present the library. A substantial percentage of the library's clientele are community residents, some of whom require very different service approaches than those designed for academic users.

Encompassing these diverse internal and external responsibilities requires special skills. In preparation for professional recruitment, the ASU West librarians identified the following characteristics of a librarian's responsibilities in our environment and organization, and defined the personal strengths and abilities that are important to successful job performance:

- Because each librarian is responsible for creating, developing and implementing a liaison relationship and program of services that are appropriate to assigned disciplines and faculty, being self directed, organized, and able to set priorities and to delegate were high on the list.
- To play an effective partnership role with faculty externally and in the affairs of the library internally, a librarian must be assertive in seizing opportunities and capable of establishing and maintaining credibility with faculty and library colleagues.
- For all of the emphasis on individuality, library services are delivered through an elaborate structure of interdependence. Therefore, a librarian must be flexible, supportive of colleagues, and capable of collaborative working relationships.
- As a participant in shaping a new institution, a librarian needs to be astute and adept at maneuvering in internal and external politics.
- Change is the only constant in our environment. Our academic programs are rapidly growing and changing, as is the nature of libraries, both locally and nationally. Therefore, a librarian needs to be versatile and creative in the application of professional skills and knowledge as well as in problem solving.

DIVIDENDS

This article has thus far been true to its title by addressing the costs of our investment in partnership. What about the dividends?

- Each of us has been stretched, personally and professionally, and we have discovered that we possessed greater skills and abilities than we knew.
- Each of us has a better understanding and appreciation of the individual components of the academic enterprise and a more holistic view of the academy.

- Each of us has a better understanding and appreciation of our colleagues—or partners—the faculty.
- Each of us knows, with vivid clarity, what the library and we as individuals contribute to the whole.
- Our jobs are never routine, never boring, and there are always more opportunities than time.
- Each of us has experienced the "high" of an uncommon level of appreciation and recognition for what we contribute.
- Kudos are more common than complaints.
- The institution takes great pride in its library, and that pride is reflected in support.

The institution also benefits:

- Library services, policies, procedures and personnel are more responsive and can incorporate diversity in accordance to need.

  Faculty enjoy a level and comprehensiveness of service that increases their productivity and helps them to achieve greater quality.
- Students lose their apprehension as a result of our user orientation and investment in teaching.
- Collections are built on the basis of direct personal knowledge of curriculum and teaching emphasis.

THE FUTURE

A partnership is not to be entered into lightly. When we speak of partnership in the academic enterprise, we normally think of shared participation and benefits, but to acquire such partnership requires investment; for librarians, that investment is comprised of time, personal skills and professional knowledge. And, sharing the risks and accountability for outcomes is a corollary to sharing the rewards.

The more successful and secure the venture, the higher the price of becoming a partner. Academic institutions have flourished for centuries without librarians as partners, so the investment that we will need to make is therefore substantial.

The higher the investment, the longer it takes to recoup. That is especially true in academe, where financial rewards are controlled by traditions that are not easily ignored by a single institution. Even the non-fiscal dividends may be slow in coming because our partnership is slowly won and even more slowly acknowledged.

A true partnership is entered into by the mutual agreement of two or more parties, and the terms of the partnership are carefully defined. If this definition is applied, then we at ASU West cannot claim to have achieved a full partnership. We still must educate and persuade in order to gain participation, and the terms of our participation are still ambiguous and inconsistent.

Rewards and accountability are other matters that remain unresolved. True partners expect to share equally the rewards and the liabilities of their endeavor. Our librarians are a long way from enjoying an equal share of the rewards, but neither are we equally liable for the quality of education that students receive or the ranking of academic programs, or the level of outside funding that the institution attracts.

Given the real and appropriate limitations of our role, we have concluded that we are investing in a limited partnership: we get a fair return of the profits and rewards of a successful academic program without either encroaching upon the interests of our faculty co-investors or assuming risks and liabilities out of proportion to our investment. Recognition of our interest in the joint enterprise of educating students, maintaining the quality of programs, and setting the research agenda is an attractive inducement to risk the price.

BIBLIOGRAPHY

American Library Association Presidential Committee on Information Literacy, *Final Report* (Chicago: ALA, 1989).

Patricia Senn Breivik and Robert Wedgeworth, *Libraries and the Search for Academic Excellence* (Metuchen: Scarecrow, 1988).

Charles B. Lowry, "An Interview with Peter F. Drucker," *Library Administration & Management* 3 (Winter 1989): 3-5.

D.J. Smith, "An Examination of Higher Education: A View from the College Library," *The Journal of Academic Librarianship* 15 (July 1989): 140-146.

Anne Woodsworth, Nancy Allen, Irene Hoadley, June Lester, Pat Molholt, Danuta Nitecki, and Lou Wetherbee, "The Model Research Library: Planning for the Future," *The Journal of Academic Librarianship* 15 (July 1989): 132-138.

Beyond Tomorrow: The Scholar, Libraries and the Dissemination of Information

Irene Hoadley
Sherrie Schmidt

SUMMARY. Libraries have made progress toward the development of the electronic library as defined by Pat Battin in 1984. As the electronic library presently exists it closely resembles an automated version of traditional library services. Before the development of the electronic library is concluded questions need to be posed and answered regarding the use of this tool. It must be ascertained whether scholars in different disciplines use automated tools in profoundly different ways in order that the electronic library meets the needs of those whom we intend to serve.

INTRODUCTION

There are many current assumptions about how scholars use information in advancing and adding to knowledge. Both librarians and scholars make those assumptions. All are valid at a minimum from a single perspective, but there are many questions which have not yet been asked. Therefore there are more hypotheses which can still be made and tested which will help to formulate the future of information systems in order to enhance the advancement of knowledge. This paper will support a definition of the electronic library, report on the status of development in relation to the definition, and suggest actions as well as questions for further study.

Irene Hoadley is Director of Libraries and Sherrie Schmidt is Assistant Director for Collection and Bibliographic Services at Texas A&M University, College Station, TX.

ELECTRONIC LIBRARY DEFINED

In order to explore the congruence of the scholar/scientist with the electronic library, it is necessary to have a shared understanding of this information system. DeGennaro in 1984 suggested that the "goal for a research library in the next decade is to plan and implement a comprehensive program for using computer and communications technologies to add a powerful new electronic dimension to supplement and enhance its traditional collections and services."[1] The efforts of libraries during the past six years indicate that this is a direction which has been embraced and that progress has been made. A more detailed specification of functions was provided by Battin. For the purpose of providing a measuring stick let us assume that the electronic library continues to evolve as described by Patricia Battin in her 1984 article in the EDUCOM *Bulletin* and that the various financial, copyright, organizational and standardization issues which operate as potential obstacles to her vision of the library of the future are avoided or negotiated. "The Electronic Scholar of the '90s will find the following opportunities at the workstation: online gateway access to the universe of knowledge; bibliographic data for all printed works and machine-readable data bases and files; extremely user-friendly access by natural language subject searching, keywords, titles, etc.; boolean logic, call-number searching, backward and forward browsing; and information on on-order and circulation status of documents."[2] The electronic library will provide the following: "downloading capacities and local interactive manipulation of all files; full text access to databases, data files and published works also preserved on optical disk; high resolution graphics; capacity to order off-line prints of machine-readable text, facsimile transmission of journal articles identified through on-line abstracting and indexing services and/or delivery of printed publications; links to printed works through on-line indexes of books, tables of contents; access to on-line Pre-print Exchange, with papers maintained on-line for six months and then purged unless referred and preserved in an archival record according to scholarly standards; the refereeing process would be coordinated by a national network of scholarly societies with accepted data sets being maintained at the home institution and entered into the national data resource—either RLIN or OCLC now linked into one national resource; (and) on-line access to education, training and consulting services run by the Scholarly Information Center, (which provides) information on new services and access, technical information on hardware, software, etc., tutorials and consulting services on literature structures, protocols for specialists, seminar for beginners, (and) literature search services for those who don't want to do their own."[3] While this or any definition of the future electronic library is arguable, it does provide one point of departure for crystal ball gazing so that we can create a scenario for the future.

Given the definition, let us measure our progress in the development of the electronic library. It is possible to begin this process by citing the utilization and acceptance of those segments which currently exist in isolation. First, the introduction of online catalogs was met with tentative acceptance, concern and high expectations for further refinement of such systems. Despite the initial limitations of online catalogs, the incompleteness and questionable quality of the bibliographic data, the proportion of records in machine-readable form versus bibliographic records represented only in the card catalog, and the restricted search strategies available, there are increasing numbers of users of this tool. The fears of some librarians that users who were excited by technology would use these restricted tools to the exclusion of more complete records were not unfounded. Nevertheless, with the continued development of online catalog systems and the concentration on retrospective conversion, online catalogs are coming closer to representing all of the items which the card catalog contained. The online catalog has become an acceptable, if not enhanced, replacement for the card catalog. Additional information such as circulation status and acquisition information is available in some online catalogs. It should be noted that the online catalog, with the exception of the power of keyword and boolean searching, is not far removed from the tool which it was designed to replace. In most cases it is no more than an automated version of the manual file.

A second component of the electronic library currently available in isolation is online abstracting and indexing services. The use and acceptance of these services both by scholars and students at Texas A&M has been inhibited only by one's ability to pay for them. In the 15 years since online searching has been available at Texas A&M, searches have increased from 280 to the peak in 1986 of 14,953. In part this increase is attributable to the availability of more databases and the availability of full or partial subsidies for searching. In general, it had been the experience at Texas A&M that scholars were not willing to do their own searching; rather they preferred to have trained searchers provide this service although "user-friendly" access has begun to change this approach. Once again, it should be noted that online indexing and abstracting services, while labor and time-saving devices, even with the increased specificity of searching possible, produce a product which is not far removed from the product which was created from paper abstracts and indexes.

Since the publication of Battin's article, the development of indexes on CD-ROM has provided another mechanism for the identification of pertinent information. The adoption and utilization of this tool by Texas A&M users would seem to support the notion that "user-friendly" access does encourage users to do their own searching. With the introduction of twenty-one CD-ROM workstations at Texas A&M, the requirement for mediated searches of external databases decreased from a high of 14,953 in 1985/86 to 10,128 in 1986/87.

Document delivery, a third component of the electronic library, is also in a state of evolution. Libraries have provided document delivery service for many years. The mode of transmission has moved from the actual piece to photocopies to telefacsimiles and to electronic files. Even though telefacsimile technology has been available for almost twenty years, it is only now that it is being readily accepted and utilized by libraries as a means of improving access for the library user. There are now telefacsimile networks to speed the delivery of information. In most cases there is a cost to the user, but that is also beginning to change as the mode of delivery becomes less of an issue.

Some of the other components mentioned by Battin are also becoming realities. Workstations are increasing both in libraries and in faculty offices and dormitory rooms. There are campus networks which provide access to a variety of information resources, and there are gateways to multiple databases to ease the complexities of searching. From some of these services it is possible to download searches onto disks.

As we can see, the initial components that Battin included as part of the electronic library exist today, but they do not exist in combination. If the parts are available, why have they not been combined into a working electronic library? Is some part still missing which has been overlooked, or is there a more fundamental issue? In brief, a multiplicity of tasks still need to be done to complete Battin's vision of the electronic library.

ALTERNATIVE VIEWS

At the same time that libraries have been moving toward Battin's definition other voices see the future from different perspectives. Bacon, in looking at the future of information development and dissemination, sees a shift from the institution to the individual. He sees portability and communications as removing constraints in the availability and dissemination of information. It will be the end user not the disseminator who will control the development of how information is conveyed, and this in turn will determine how knowledge based institutions are reshaped.[4]

This scenario, which many librarians describe in terms of how scholars use information, implies that many individuals presently have their own subscriptions to commercial databases and are busily doing their own searching and research, thereby by-passing the campus library.

One implication of this view is that if faculty pursue doing their own database (bibliographic, numeric and full text) searching, then the campus cost of information moves from the library to the individual or an academic unit. In such a case, the library would not be responsible for these costs because they are beyond its control. Another implication of this view of the future involves the time factor. Is a faculty member or his/her graduate assistant going to take the time to learn one or maybe multiple systems to access the necessary databases? And once the systems are learned, will the individual maintain enough proficiency to be able to search with relative ease? Will the faculty member want to deal with billings and other administrative procedures in this searching process?

To assess the probability of this view of the future being accurate, data is needed to be able to determine what faculty are really doing now as well as their perceptions of how they want to access information in the future. A preliminary study has been undertaken at Texas A&M to determine whether faculty are doing their own searching and if so whether they use the resources of the library or their own personal resources. Although the study has not been completed it appears that about half of the faculty who responded are doing their own searching.[5] If the final results verify this preliminary finding and if the study can be replicated at other institutions to verify the results, then this would be significant information for libraries to use in planning access services for the future.

What if the library continues to be the major purveyor of campus information? Is the present situation of mediated and end-user bibliographic searching and dial-in-access to the online catalog adequate as the way that future scholars will access information? Probably not since these technologies do not even meet the needs of today's scholars. But what is needed? What would seem most advantageous to the humanities faculty is a single access device tied to a campus network with appropriate gateways to allow access to the online catalog (which includes books, journals, government documents, microforms, audiovisuals, and manuscripts/archival holdings) as well as any locally mounted files and commercial databases.

The scientist's needs, on the other hand, are a little different. The scientist has less interest in the online catalog but has more need for journal bibliographical databases as well as numeric and full text to be able to determine that an item is really what is wanted. In addition, this individual will also want document delivery or a printing facility to actually obtain the document without leaving his/her office. There are already scholars who are proposing such electronic libraries and who are concerned that libraries are not moving in this direction. Again in some cases, these scholars are developing their own mechanisms including gateways which will bypass the library.[6]

Many who view the library as the major provider of campus information see a changing role for the librarians. There are those who see the role of the librarian as a "facilitator who provides access to terminals, instruction, and guidance in choosing the best system for the task at hand.'"[7] The emphasis here is on the scholar performing the searches and choosing the appropriate information rather than the librarian fulfilling the role of intermediary. The implication of this scenario is that the role of the librarian really is that of teaching and guiding rather than doing.

Beyond the basic issues of determining how scholars use information depending on the discipline, there is one other large unknown. As time has moved forward so has the availability of written information/documentation. Every librarian is aware of the "information explosion" that has overtaken our organizations. As more and more information is available, there will be a greater need to provide some type of content analysis to facilitate retrieving appropriate information. What is already happening is that there is so much information on any one topic that it is difficult to be thorough in doing bibliographical research. There must be an approach developed that allows us to do comprehensive searches while still being able to obtain more specific information.

So far our point of departure then for moving toward the electronic library has been defined by our current progress toward Battin's definition of it. The next steps must help us move beyond tomorrow to our goal of the complete electronic library.

MOVING TOWARD OUR FUTURE

Libraries must take an active role in initiating and controlling the changes which must occur for the electronic library to become a reality. Libraries have been tested by external change almost since their beginnings. There were and are several choices for dealing with change: to ignore external changes; to incorporate external changes; to modify the changes for library purposes. Among the choices which have to be made, there is probably no right or wrong choice, but simply a matter of degrees. The important point then becomes what is the effect of the decision that is made and how does the decision help the library move forward or, at minimum, assure that the library maintains the status quo in a changing world.

Unfortunately, more often than not, libraries have not been concerned with shaping the future. For the most part, libraries have allowed external changes to shape what they do because they fail to make choices. If libraries are to survive as meaningful organizations, they must involve themselves in the decision-making process. The first step then in taking an active role in determining the future is to develop a vision of the electronic library. One such view has already been defined in terms of this paper. Once that vision or goal has been articulated, it will be a lot easier to make the other decisions which will achieve the desired result.

But as we have seen being able to determine the final configuration for an electronic library is not an easy task. It assumes a certain amount of knowledge of technology, an awareness of the campus environment, a willingness to take some risks and some thought. Risk taking is not high in the repertoire of librarians. However, if some risks are not taken, then the external forces are more apt to do the shaping rather than the library controlling the environment. There will be two deterents to innovation—money and attitude. The problem of money can be solved, but the question of attitude may be more difficult to overcome.

Once there is a focus, a goal to attain, a definition agreed upon, that first step has been taken, but this is only the beginning. There is also a need for several other factors to be in place to encourage innovation and to move the process forward. The first is an environment that is open to change, both within the library and the university. In general, libraries have changed a lot in the past two decades, but if those changes are examined closely what one sees is the same functions but executed in more sophisticated ways. Libraries have automated their manual systems rather than being more analytical and determining how they can enhance the research process. But even to automate manual systems has taken much effort, many dollars and a lot of time. Furthermore, not all libraries have been able to move as quickly into the electronic age. For example, some libraries have provided mediated database searching for fifteen years while for some it is a service initiated in the past three to five years. There are still many libraries that continue to do their own cataloging rather than participate in a bibliographic utility or buy their cataloging from a vendor. These examples are indicative of the points on the spectrum where libraries are. It is important to understand that each library does not begin at the same point or operate in the same environment. But regardless of where a library begins, what is needed is an environment that not only accepts change but even promotes it. How does this happen? It begins with leadership, but it also requires a staff who are interested in providing the ultimate in service both in terms of what is available and in terms of quality. It is only by striving for more than is available or presently possible that gives one the impetus to continue to move forward to the next level. That need to do more is what lays the ground work for an environment which promotes change.

A second factor which must be present for an electronic library to be successful is standards. Everyone is familiar with the current situation on campuses where computing in all of its manifestations has sprung up in response to a variety of needs. The end result is a range of hardware and software which, in many instances, handles a single function for a specific individual or group. So far networking of hardware and software has not always been a primary concern. However, if an electronic library is to be an integral part of campus computing, there must be standards to allow the various computing resources to interact.

Standards can be approached on several levels. The most advantageous is national standards to which producers conform so that different types of hardware can at least communicate with each other. Interchangeability is desirable but not always practical from the producer's point of view. Interfaces which provide the ability for interaction through telecommunications is probably the most viable option for computing in general and specifically for integrated library systems. The ability for a variety of hardware to be connected over telecommunication lines to one or more databases will provide a user the opportunity from a personal terminal to access a number of campus information resources, as well as many resources beyond the campus. However, this cannot happen without standards for the hardware, the software and telecommunications protocols.

A third factor which must be present to enhance the viability of an electronic library is the presence of incentives. Why are incentives necessary for the successful implementation of an electronic library? The electronic library is a new concept for the academic campus which is not known to embrace new ideas with great willingness. To see this all one must consider the process of teaching which has not changed since the time of Socrates. Faculty members still impart facts to an assembled group of students. Since faculty are a group that do not embrace change readily, this means that there must be some impetus to have faculty accept a new way to obtain information.

There are several alternatives for encouraging faculty participation. The first is to make it easy. This could mean that all faculty are provided with the necessary hardware and software to access the available information resources. It would also be necessary to insure that faculty have the expertise to utilize these resources, but it will be imperative that this be done in a non-threatening way. A second alternative is to require participation by eliminating other options. The removal of the card catalog is one example of eliminating other options. A third option is to encourage developments of alternative interfaces for using these new resources. Interfaces for the frequent and experienced user as well as the inexperienced and infrequent user will be necessary. Finally, acceptance will also be enhanced by involving faculty in the development of the electronic library and its integration into the campus network.

CONCLUSION

The first question that should be raised, then, as we plan for the future, is will this concept of the electronic library provide the proper environment and resources for scholars to pursue their quest for knowledge? Is our definition of the electronic library going to facilitate the research process? If the process does not change much from what it is today, then there is a good chance the library will be successful in its effort.

On the other hand, do libraries really know if they are contributing to the present scholarly process? The profession continues to make those assumptions, but there has not been much research to verify the assumptions. Before libraries commit to a specific future it would be advantageous to know more about the intellectual exchange of information in a broad range of disciplines. Rather than doing things right, we need to determine if we are doing the right things.

An electronic library is only one step towards the future. But as each step moves us forward, there is also the necessity to maintain some of the past. Libraries are often like sponges in that they continue to add more and more to what they do. In the transition stages, it is not a case of putting the old aside for the new. The old and new must coexist, creating a juxtaposition of manual and automated processes. This makes the role of the library and librarians more difficult in that it requires a staff and resources to handle two systems and to provide an environment which will allow users to progress at a rate that matches their expertise and at the same time anticipates the future. If librarians do not continue to move forward, and to seek answers to the questions posed here, they may well be left out of the future information environment.

NOTES

1. DeGennaro, Richard, "Shifting Gears: Information Technology and the Academic Library," *Library Journal*, (June 15, 1984), 1206.
2. Patricia Battin, "The Electronic Library—A Vision of the Future," *EDUCOM Bulletin*, (vol. 19, no.2) p. 17.
3. *Ibid.*, 17, 34.
4. Bacon, Glenn C., "Forces Shaping the New Information Paradigm." In: Edelman, Hendrick. *Libraries and Information Science in the Electronic Age.* Philadelphia: ISI Press, 1986, pp. 162-163.
5. Gomez, Joni and Katy Clark.
6. Weiskel, Timothy C., "The Electronic Library," *Change* (November/December 1988), 38-47.
7. Lewis, David W., "Inventing the Electronic University," *College and Research Libraries* 49 (July 1988), 297.

For Product Safety Concerns and Information please contact our EU
representative GPSR@taylorandfrancis.com
Taylor & Francis Verlag GmbH, Kaufingerstraße 24, 80331 München, Germany

www.ingramcontent.com/pod-product-compliance
Lightning Source LLC
Chambersburg PA
CBHW052133300426
44116CB00010B/1882